Rational Emotive Behaviour Therapy:
Learning from
Demonstration Sessions

Rational Emotive Behaviour Therapy: Learning from Demonstration Sessions

Windy Dryden

Goldsmiths College, London

W

Whurr Publishers

© 1996 Whurr Publishers
19b Compton Terrace, London N1 2UN, England

British Library Cataloguing in Publication Data
A catalogue record for this book is available from the
British Library.

ISBN 1-897635-44-3

Printed and bound in the UK by Athenaeum Press Ltd,
Gateshead, Tyne & Wear

Contents

Acknowledgements

I would like to thank the following:

'Linda' and 'Susan' for giving their permission for their interviews to be transcribed and published in this volume.

Albert Ellis for providing a commentary on his interview with Susan.

Sage Publications for granting permission for me to publish Chapter 1, which is a modified version of the introduction to *Developing Rational Emotive Behavioural Counselling*, written by Windy Dryden and Joseph Yankura (1995).

Whurr Publishers for granting permission for me to publish Chapter 2, which is a modified version of Chapter 9 in *Counselling Individuals: A Rational-Emotive Handbook*, written by Windy Dryden and Joseph Yankura (1993).

Introduction

The purpose of the 'Practical Skills in Rational Emotive Behaviour Therapy' series is to provide training material for new trainees in REBT. In this volume, I provide a transcript of two demonstration sessions of REBT, one conducted by Albert Ellis and the other conducted by myself. Both of these demonstration sessions were conducted during introductory training courses on REBT. A feature of this book is the commentary that is provided to help you to understand the reasons for the therapist's interventions.

To put the demonstration sessions and the associated commentaries in context, in Chapter 1 I provide a short introduction to the theory and practice of REBT and in Chapter 2 I outline the 13 steps of the REBT treatment sequence. An understanding of the latter is crucial if you are to get the most out of the transcripts and commentaries.

On introductory training courses in REBT, trainees watch and listen to demonstration sessions of REBT in their entirety before discussing their observations. To approximate this sequence, I first present each demonstration session before reproducing it again with an ongoing commentary. While the transcripts are an accurate record of the demonstration sessions, I have made changes where relevant to make the dialogue more comprehensible.

Let me make one point clear, both clients have given written permission for the transcript of their interview to be published in this book. To safeguard their anonymity, I have changed all identifiable material.

Finally, this book is best used as part of a comprehensive training package in REBT. In particular it should be read in conjunction with other books in this series (Dryden, 1995a,b).

Chapter 1
The Basic Principles
and Practice of Rational
Emotive Behaviour
Therapy

In this opening chapter, I will cover the basic principles of REBT. In particular, I will consider (1) REBT's specific principle of emotional responsibility; (2) the two types of psychological disturbance; (3) the principle of psychological interactionism; and (4) the process of therapeutic change. I will also introduce the now famous 'ABCDE's of REBT.

REBT's Specific Principle of Emotional Responsibility

Epictetus, the famous Roman philosopher, once said that people are disturbed not by events, but by the views they take of these events. This statement is at the heart of the cognitive theory of emotional disturbance, but is too vague for REBT. The specific principle of emotional responsibility that is at the heart of REBT is so termed because it specifies precisely the kinds of 'views' that are at the core of psychological disturbance and, as importantly, the kinds of 'views' that are at the core of psychological well-being. In outlining the REBT position on this issue, I will present four belief pairs. The first belief in any pair will be that associated with psychological health and the second will be that associated with psychological disturbance. In the language of REBT, the first is known as a rational belief and the second as an irrational belief. Before I present the four belief pairs that describe precisely how we disturb ourselves about self, others and life conditions and what we would have to think to be healthy instead, let me briefly discuss the terms 'rational' and 'irrational' as they are used in REBT theory.

Rational and irrational

The term 'rational' in REBT theory refers to beliefs that are (1) flexible;

3

(2) consistent with reality; (3) logical; and that (4) promote the person's psychological well-being and aid her pursuit of her personally meaningful goals. In contrast, the term 'irrational' in REBT theory refers to beliefs that are (1) rigid; (2) inconsistent with reality; (3) illogical; and that (4) interfere with the person's psychological well-being and get in the way of her pursuing her personally meaningful goals.

The four belief pairs

Preferences vs musts. Rational beliefs are flexible in nature and are often couched in the form of preferences (or its synonyms, e.g. wishes, wants, desires, etc.). Preferences can point to what we want to happen (e.g. 'I want to pass my driving test') or to what we don't not want to occur (e.g. 'I don't want to get into trouble with my boss'). However, to understand the full meaning of a preference, its non-dogmatic nature needs to be made explicit in the person's statement. To take the two examples I have just mentioned, we can tell that they are really preferences thus:

> 'I want to pass my driving test, BUT I don't have to do so.'
> 'I don't want to get into trouble with my boss, BUT there's no reason why I must not do so.'

The reason why it is so important for a preference to be phrased in its full form is that if it is expressed in its partial form (e.g. 'I want to pass my driving test'), then it is easy for us to change it implicitly to a dogmatic must (e.g. 'I want to pass my driving test (and therefore I have to do so)'). Indeed, the stronger our preferences, the more likely we are, if left to our own devices, to change these preferences into musts.

Preferences are rational because they are (1) flexible (i.e. they allow for what is not preferred to occur); (2) consistent with reality (i.e. they are consistent with the inner reality of the person's preferences); (3) logical; and they (4) promote the person's psychological well-being and aid her pursuit of her personally meaningful goals (i.e. they lead to healthy negative emotions when the person's preferences are not met, which in turn facilitate effective problem-solving or constructive adjustment if changes cannot be made).

Irrational beliefs are rigid in nature and are often couched in the form of musts (or its synonyms, e.g. absolute shoulds, have to's, got to's, etc.). Musts indicate that we believe that what we want absolutely has to occur (e.g. 'I absolutely have to pass my driving test') or that what we do not want absolutely should not happen (e.g. 'I must not get into trouble with my boss').

Musts are irrational because they are (1) inflexible (i.e. they do not allow for what must happen not to occur); (2) inconsistent with reality (i.e. they are inconsistent with reality; if there was a law of the universe that says I must pass my driving test, I could not possibly fail. This law, of course, does not exist); (3) illogical (i.e. they do not logically follow on from the person's preferences); and they (4) interfere with the person's psychological well-being and get in the way of her pursuing her personally meaningful goals (i.e. they lead to unhealthy negative emotions when the person's demands are not met, which in turn impede effective problem-solving or constructive adjustment if changes cannot be made).

Albert Ellis (1994), the founder of REBT, holds that non-dogmatic preferences are at the very core of psychological health and that three other major rational beliefs are derived from these preferences. Similarly, Ellis believes that dogmatic musts are at the very core of emotional disturbance and that three other irrational beliefs are derived from these musts.

Anti-awfulizing vs awfulizing. Anti-awfulizing beliefs are rational in the sense that they are first and foremost non-dogmatic. These beliefs, which in their full form are expressed thus: 'It would be very bad if I failed my driving test, BUT it wouldn't be awful', are flexibly located on a continuum in the range of 0–99.99% badness. The stronger a person's unmet preference, the higher her evaluation will be placed on this continuum. However, an anti-awfulizing belief cannot reach 100%, since as Smokey Robinson's mother used to tell her young son: 'From the time you are born 'till you ride in the hearse, there's nothing so bad that it couldn't be worse.' In this sense, an anti-awfulizing belief is consistent with reality. This belief is also logical in that it makes sense in the context of the person's preference. Finally, it is constructive for it will help the person take effective action if the negative event that the person is facing can be changed and it will aid the person to make a healthy adjustment if the situation cannot be changed.

Awfulizing beliefs, on the other hand, are irrational in the sense that they are first and foremost dogmatic. They are rigidly located on a magical 'horror' continuum ranging from 101% badness to infinity. They are couched in such statements as 'It's horrible that...', 'It's terrible that...', 'It's awful that...' and 'It's the end of the world that...' When a person is awfulizing, he literally believes at that moment that nothing could be worse. In this sense, an awfulizing belief is inconsistent with reality. This belief is also illogical because it is a nonsensical conclusion from the person's implicit rational belief (e.g. 'Because it would would be very bad if I failed my driving test it would therefore be awful if this happened'). Finally, it is unconstructive in that it will interfere with the person taking effective action if the negative event that the person is facing can be changed and it will stop the person making a healthy adjustment if the situation cannot be changed.

High frustration tolerance (HFT) vs low frustration tolerance (LFT).
High frustration tolerance beliefs are rational in the sense that they are
again primarily flexible and not grossly exaggerated. These beliefs are
expressed in their full form, thus: 'Failing my driving test would be difficult to tolerate, BUT I could stand it.' The stronger a person's unmet
preference, the more difficult it would be for her to tolerate this situation, but if she holds an HFT belief it would still be tolerable. In this
sense, an HFT belief is consistent with reality. It is also logical since it
again makes sense in the context of the person's preference. Finally,
like a preference and an anti-awfulizing belief, it is constructive since it
will help the person take effective action if the negative event that the
person is facing can be changed and it will aid the person to make a
healthy adjustment if the situation cannot be changed.

Low frustration tolerance beliefs, on the other hand, are irrational in
the sense that they are first and foremost grossly exaggerated. They are
couched in such statements as 'I can't stand it...', 'I can't bear it...', 'It's
intolerable...' When a person has a low frustration tolerance belief, she
means one of two things: (1) she will disintegrate or (2) she will never
experience any happiness again. Since these two statements are obviously untrue, an LFT belief is inconsistent with reality. It is also illogical
since it is a nonsensical conclusion from the person's implicit rational
belief (e.g. 'Because failing my driving test would be difficult for me to
tolerate, I couldn't stand it if I did fail'). Finally, like musts and awfulizing beliefs, it is unconstructive since it will interfere with the person
taking effective action if the negative event that the person is facing can
be changed and it will stop the person making a healthy adjustment if
the situation cannot be changed.

Self/other acceptance vs self/other downing. Acceptance beliefs are
rational in the sense that they are again primarily flexible. In discussing
acceptance beliefs, I will focus on self-acceptance, although exactly the
same arguments apply to other-acceptance. When a person accepts herself, she acknowledges that she is a unique, ongoing, ever-changing fallible human being with good, bad and neutral aspects. In short, she is
far too complex to merit a single, global rating. Self-esteem, on the
other hand is based on the idea that it is possible to assign a single rating to the 'self'. An example of a self-acceptance belief expressed in its
full form follows: 'If I fail my driving test due to my own errors, I could
still accept myself as a fallible human being who has failed on this occa-
sion. I would not be a failure.' As this example shows, a self-acceptance
belief is consistent with the reality of a person being too complex to
merit a single global rating. A self-acceptance belief is also logical since
it is logical for a person to conclude that he is fallible if he makes
errors. Finally, as with the other three rational beliefs I have discussed, a
self-acceptance belief is constructive since it will once again help the

person take effective action if the negative event that the person is facing can be changed and it will also aid the person to make a healthy adjustment if the situation cannot be changed.

Self-downing beliefs, on the other hand, are irrational in the sense that they take a rigid, grossly exaggerated view of the 'self'. They are couched in such statements as 'I am bad', 'I am a failure', 'I am less worthy', 'I am undeserving'. When a person holds a self-downing belief, he is working on the assumption that it is legitimate to assign a global (in this case, negative) rating to his 'self'. Since this in fact cannot be legitimately done, a self-downing belief is inconsistent with reality. It is also illogical since in making a self-downing statement, the person is making the 'part-whole error', i.e. he is correctly rating an aspect of himself, but then he rates his entire self based on the evaluation of the part. Finally, like the other three irrational beliefs I have discussed, a self-downing belief is unconstructive since it will interfere with the person taking effective action if the negative event that the person is facing can be changed and it will stop the person making a healthy adjustment if the situation cannot be changed.

Having now introduced the four rational beliefs and four irrational beliefs deemed by REBT theory to lie at the core of psychological well-being and psychological disturbance respectively, let us formally state the specific principle of emotional responsibility:

> The REBT specific principle of emotional responsibility states that events contribute to the way we feel and act, but do not cause these reactions which are largely determined by our rational or irrational beliefs about these events.

The Two Types of Psychological Disturbance

Having outlined the four irrational beliefs that underpin psychological disturbance, we will now proceed to discuss the two different types of such disturbance: Ego disturbance and discomfort disturbance.

Ego disturbance

As the name implies, ego disturbance concerns psychological problems that ultimately relate to the person's view of herself. Sometimes such problems are obviously related to the self as when a person is depressed and says, almost without prompting: 'Because I failed my driving test, I am a failure.' At other times, ego disturbance is not so transparent. For example, a person might claim to be anxious about travelling by Underground. Put like that, it is not at all obvious that the person's problem may be an example of ego disturbance. However, on much closer examination, this turns out to be the case when the person reveals that he is anxious about travelling by Tube because he might get panicky and, as stated in his own words, 'I would make a fool of myself by passing out.' Effective REBT is based on an accurate assessment of a client's problems and this assessment will reveal whether or not a particular problem is related to ego disturbance.

As discussed above, ego disturbance occurs when a person makes a global, negative rating of his or her self. Such ratings can be made in different areas and are related to different disorders. Let us provide a few examples to illustrate our point:

1. When a person believes that she is a failure or a loser then it is likely that she will be depressed when she has failed or anxious when there exists a threat of failure which hasn't yet occurred.
2. When a person believes that she is bad then it is likely that she will experience guilt.
3. When a person believes that she is defective or weak then it is likely that she will experience shame.

The self-ratings that are involved in ego disturbance are usually expressed quite starkly as in the statements: 'I am bad' or 'I am a bad person'. However, they can also be expressed more subtly as in the statements: 'I am less worthy' or 'I am undeserving'. Generally speaking, the more starkly they are expressed in the person's belief structure, the greater that person's ego disturbance will be.

Finally, as noted above, ego disturbance is derived from dogmatic musturbatory beliefs as in the following example: 'I am a failure because I did not pass my driving test as I absolutely should have done.' According to this view, if the person in this example had a preferential belief about failing, such as: 'I would have preferred not to have failed my driving test, but there's no reason why I absolutely should not have done', then she would be far less likely to condemn herself than she would if she held a demanding belief about failure as shown at the beginning of this paragraph.

Discomfort disturbance

As the name implies, discomfort disturbance concerns psychological problems that ultimately relate to the person's sense of comfort and discomfort. In REBT, the concepts of comfort and discomfort cover a wide range of issues. For example, they may relate to justice/injustice, fulfilment/frustration, positive feelings/negative feelings, etc. What they have in common, however, is they do not refer to the person's view of himself. Rather, as the name implies concerns discomfort disturbance relates to the person's perceived inability to tolerate discomfort, whether this is in the area of feelings (e.g. anxiety) or life situations (e.g. unfairness).

Like ego disturbance, discomfort disturbance can be obvious or more subtle. An example of discomfort disturbance that is obvious is when a person says that she cannot stand waiting for the traffic lights to change. A more subtle example of discomfort disturbance is when a person says that she is afraid of failing her driving test. It might appear, at first sight, that the person's anxiety is an example of ego disturbance. However, on much closer examination, this turns out not to be the case when the person reveals that she is anxious about not getting the thousand pounds that her father promised her if she passed the test. As she said, 'I couldn't bear to lose out on all the goodies I had planned to buy with the money.' This is clearly an example of discomfort disturbance. As I mentioned earlier, careful assessment is needed to tease out discomfort disturbance-related irrational beliefs.

Discomfort disturbance occurs when a person has LFT beliefs. Such beliefs can be held in different areas and are related to different disorders. Let me provide a few examples to illustrate my point:

1. When a person believes that she cannot stand being blocked or frustrated then it is likely that she will be angry.
2. When a person believes that she cannot tolerate losing a prized possession then it is likely that she will experience depression if she lost it.
3. When a person believes that she can't bear feeling anxious then it is likely that she will experience increased anxiety.

The evaluations that are involved in discomfort disturbance can be explicit as when the person says that she cannot bear the discomfort of speaking in public. However, they can also be implicit as when people avoid facing uncomfortable situations. It is as if the person is implicitly saying: 'I'll avoid that situation because I couldn't stand the discomfort of facing it.' The more widespread the person's avoidance, the greater that person's discomfort disturbance is likely to be.

Finally, as noted above, discomfort disturbance is derived from dogmatic musturbatory beliefs as in the following example: 'I can't stand being deprived because I absolutely must get what I want.' As discussed in the section on ego disturbance, if the person in this example had a preferential belief about being deprived such as: 'I would like to get what I want, but I don't have to get it', then she would be far less likely to disturb herself about the deprivation than she would if she held a demanding belief about her failure to get what she wants.

Ego disturbance and discomfort disturbance can interact

Ego disturbance and discomfort disturbance can interact, often in complex ways. For example, let's suppose that a person believes that she must do well at a job interview and if she does not that means that she is less worthy than she would be if she did well. This ego disturbance belief leads the person to feel anxiety as the date of the interview draws near. At this point the person becomes aware that she is feeling anxious and tells herself implicitly that she must get rid of her anxiety straight away and that she can't stand feeling anxious. As the result of this discomfort disturbance belief, her anxiety increases. Realising that she is getting very anxious for what to her is no good reason and that she absolutely shouldn't do this, she concludes that she is a weak, pathetic person for getting matters out of proportion. This ego disturbance adds to her emotional distress which activates fears discomfort-related irrational beliefs about losing control.

It is important to note that this interaction between ego disturbance and discomfort disturbance can occur very quickly and outside the person's awareness. Dealing therapeutically with complex interactions between the two types of disturbance as exemplified above is quite difficult and involves the therapist dealing with one link of the chain at a time.

The ABCDEs of REBT

You will find the ABCs of REBT in virtually every book that has been published on REBT and here I will briefly describe what this means.

A

A stands for an activating event which triggers your client's rational or irrational beliefs, which in turn determine her feelings and the way she acts. As can be actual events or inferences (i.e. hypotheses about actual events which may be correct or incorrect, but which need testing out). Furthermore, As can be external events or internal events (e.g. bodily sensations) and can stand for past, present or future events.

B

B stands for your client's rational and irrational beliefs which are evaluative in nature. I have already presented the four major types of rational and irrational beliefs as they are featured in REBT (see pp. 4–7). While some REBT therapists prefer to place all cognitive activity under B, it is my practice to put only rational and irrational beliefs under B and to put other cognitions (e.g. inferences) at A.

C

C stands for the person's emotional and/or behavioural response to the beliefs that he holds about the event (or inference) in question. In

REBT theory, negative emotions can be healthy (i.e. when they are based on rational beliefs about A) or unhealthy (i.e. when they are based on irrational beliefs about A). For further information about healthy and unhealthy negative emotions, see Chapter 2 and Dryden (1990).

It is easy to forget that C also stands for a behavioural response. Sometimes your client will exhibit self-defeating behaviour based on a set of irrational beliefs she holds about A. When this occurs either the behaviour occurs without corresponding emotion or it is designed to 'ward off' your client's disturbed feelings. This is the case in the demonstration session conducted by Albert Ellis (see Chapter 5).

D

D stands for disputing. In particular it stands for disputing your client's irrational beliefs by asking questions that encourage the person to question the empirical, logical and pragmatic status of her irrational beliefs. I will discuss disputing more fully in the next chapter.

E

E stands for the effects of disputing. When disputing is successful it helps the client to change her feelings and actions at C, and change her thinking at B. In addition, when disputing is successful, it helps the person to make more functional inferences at A.

Having spelled out the ABCDEs of REBT, I will now show how some of these interact in complex ways.

The Principle of Psychological Interactionism

So far, you can be forgiven if you think that REBT considers that thinking, feeling and behaviour are separate psychological systems. However, this is far from the case. When Albert Ellis originated REBT in the mid-1950s (which was first known as Rational Psychotherapy), he put forward the view that thinking (including imagery), feeling and behaviour are interdependent, interacting psychological processes.

Thus, when a person experiences an emotion at C, he has the tendency to think and act in a certain way. Also, when someone holds a rational or irrational belief (at B) about a negative event (at A), this will influence his feelings and behaviours (at C). Finally, if a person acts in a certain way, this will be related to his feelings and thoughts.

What follows on from this is (1) that REBT therapists need to pay close attention to thoughts, feelings and behaviour in the assessment process, and (2) that they need to use a variety of cognitive, emotive and behavioural techniques in the intervention phase of therapy.

The Process of Therapeutic Change

In order to practise REBT effectively, it is important to have an understanding of the process of therapeutic change. This knowledge will help you to use REBT interventions in the most appropriate sequence. I will briefly mention the steps that clients need to take in REBT to experience therapeutic change, before discussing each step in greater detail. While I will put these steps in a certain order, please note that this order is not a rigid one and should certainly not be applied rigidly in therapy. Also, there will be problems along the way since therapeutic change is rarely, if ever, a smooth process.

1. Understanding the specific principle of emotional responsibility.
2. Understanding the determinants of one's psychological problems.
3. Setting goals and committing oneself to achieving them.
4. Understanding and committing oneself to the REBT means of achieving one's goals.
5. Putting this learning into practice.
6. Maintaining these gains.

Understanding the specific principle of emotional responsibility

I discussed this principle at length at the beginning of this chapter, so I will not repeat myself here. However, it is important to stress that if your clients do not grasp or do not accept this principle, then they will derive little benefit from REBT.

Understanding the determinants of one's psychological problems

This step involves you and your client pooling resources to apply the specific principle of emotional responsibility to illuminate the determinants of the client's emotional problems. This involves you helping your client to specify her problems and give examples of these problems so that these can be assessed. Assessment is directed towards identifying unhealthy emotions, the actual or inferred events that provide the context for these emotions, the behaviours that the client enacts when she is experiencing her unhealthy emotions and, most importantly, the irrational beliefs that lie at the core of the client's problems. Unless your client understands the determinants of her problems and agrees with this assessment, REBT will falter at this point.

Setting goals and committing oneself to achieving them

An important part of therapeutic change is setting goals and committing time, energy and effort to taking the necessary steps to achieving them.

Let us consider each of these points in turn.

Goal-setting. There is an old adage that says: 'If you don't know where you're going, you won't know when you've got there.' This points to the importance of setting goals in the therapeutic change process. Bordin (1979) noted that agreement on therapeutic goals is an important therapeutic ingredient and one part of a tripartite view of the working alliance that has gained much prominence in psychotherapy research (Horvath and Greenberg, 1994). In REBT, you should help your client to set goals that are: specific, realistic, achievable, measurable and that aid her overall psychological well-being. Your client should 'own' her goals, which means that she should set them primarily for her own well-being and not to please anybody else (e.g. significant others or you as therapist).

However, as an REBT therapist, you have an important goal for your client and it is very important that you are open about this and discuss it frankly with her. This goal involves your client learning and practising the skills of what might be called REBT self-help counselling so that she can use them after therapy has ended. Indeed, your role as an REBT therapist is to give to your clients as much of REBT as they are able to learn. You will, of course, have to help your clients understand that learning these skills will help them to achieve their therapeutic goals, otherwise they will have little interest in learning them. As Bordin (1979) noted, helping your clients to see the relevance of your and their therapeutic tasks to achieving their goals is a central part of the process of psychotherapy and this is especially true in REBT. Not all clients will want to learn these self-help skills and you can help them (albeit less effectively) without teaching them these skills. However, if you do not offer this opportunity to your clients, they will certainly not be able to take advantage of it.

Making a commitment to achieve goals. Goal-setting will be an academic exercise unless your clients are prepared to commit themselves to achieving them. A major reason why people do not keep to their new year resolutions for very long is that they are not prepared to do what is necessary to achieve what they have resolved to achieve. They want the gain without the pain. So, as part of the goal-setting process, discuss with your clients how much time, effort and energy they will have to expend in order to achieve their goals. Then ask them if they are willing to make such an investment. If they are, then you may wish to make a formal agreement with them to this effect. If they are not prepared to make the necessary investment, then you will have to set new goals in line with the kind of investment they are prepared to make. Of course, this may all change once your work with your client has advanced. Nevertheless, it is important to get REBT off on the right foot in this respect. So, in short, set goals with your clients that they are prepared to commit to before you do any further therapy with them.

Understanding and committing to the REBT means of achieving one's goals

After you have agreed with your client goals to which she is prepared to commit herself, you then have to ensure that she understands your suggestions concerning how these goals can best be reached. This is the aspect of REBT where the technical nature of therapy comes to the fore. REBT does have definite suggestions concerning what clients need to do in order to achieve their goals. These suggestions take the form of specific techniques. In order for clients to understand the nature of REBT in this respect, you need to be able to explain what you are going to do in therapy and what is expected of your client in ways that are clear and detailed. You want clients to proceed with therapy having made an informed decision about REBT. In your description you need to stress two things. First, you need to show your client how putting into practice the technical aspects of the therapy will help her to achieve her goals. Second, you need to explain what investments with respect to time, energy and effort your client needs to make in putting REBT techniques into practice.

I have found it very useful at this juncture to point out to clients that there exist other approaches to therapy and that if what I have to offer does not make sense to the person, if she does not think that REBT will helpful to her or if she thinks it involves too much of an investment for her, then I suggest other therapeutic possibilities, discuss these with the client and make a judicious referral.

Putting this learning into practice

It is not sufficient for clients to understand that they have to put REBT techniques into practice, nor even to commit themselves to so doing. They actually have to do it. Otherwise they will have 'intellectual insight' which in this context may be seen as a light and occasionally held conviction that their irrational beliefs are irrational and their rational beliefs are rational. While this 'intellectual insight' is important to have, it is insufficient to help clients to achieve their goals. For this to occur, clients need a fair measure of what might be called 'emotional insight' which in this context is the same realisation about rational and irrational beliefs as in 'intellectual insight', but one which is strongly and frequently held. It is this 'emotional insight' which affects a person's feelings and influences his behaviour and this is the true goal of clients putting their learning into practice in their everyday lives.

There are several dimensions of between session practice that are important here.

1. *Repetition.* It is important for clients to go over new rational beliefs

many times before they begin to believe them. This repetition applies to the use of cognitive, emotive and behavioural techniques.

2. *Force and energy*. One useful way that clients can move from intellectual insight to emotional insight is to employ techniques with force and energy. However, it is important that they can understand and see the relevance of particular rational beliefs before forcefully and energetically working to internalize them.

3. *Vividness*. The use of what I have called vivid techniques in REBT (Dryden, 1986a) can help clients to remember their rational beliefs more than standard, non-vivid techniques. Vividness tends to increase the impact of rational concepts and thus makes it easier for clients to retrieve them from memory at times when it is necessary to do so. As such, they will get more practice at thinking rationally than they would ordinarily do.

Ordinarily, it is important for REBT therapists to take great care when they negotiate homework assignments with their clients. However, no matter how careful you are when negotiating such assignments, your clients may still have difficulty putting them into practice. As such, an important part of encouraging clients to put their therapy-derived insights into practice is helping them to identify and overcome such obstacles.

Maintaining therapeutic gains

Once your clients have achieved their goals, this is not the end of the therapeutic story, although many of your clients will think or hope that it is. If they have such thoughts and hopes then they will stop using the principles that you have taught them and thus increase the chances that they will experience a lapse or, more seriously, a relapse. I define a lapse as a minor return to the problem state, while a relapse is a major return to this state. If your clients are to maintain their therapeutic gains they have to be helped to so and take responsibility for this maintenance work themselves. This involves (1) relapse prevention and (2) spreading the effect of change.

Relapse prevention. It is important to deal with relapse prevention before the end of REBT, otherwise the client may not be prepared with the re-emergence of his problems. As mentioned above, it is rare for clients not to experience lapses and if they do, they need prior help to deal with a lapse when it occurs. If a lapse, or a series of lapses, is not dealt with, it may lead to a relapse since relapses tend to occur when lapses are not identified and dealt with by the person concerned. Relapse prevention, therefore, involves the following steps:

1. Recognizing that lapses are likely to occur and thinking rationally about this point.
2. Identifying the likely contexts in which lapses are likely to occur and problem-solving each salient element.
3. Exposing oneself to the problematic contexts and using the problem-solving skills previously learned to prevent the development of the lapse.
4. Committing oneself to continue this process for as long as necessary.

If the worst comes to the worst and a relapse does occur then you should help your client to think rationally about this grim reality. Understanding of how this developed should be sought before further treatment decisions are made.

If it looks unlikely that your client will achieve her therapeutic goals by the end of therapy, it is still worthwhile raising the issue of relapse prevention, although necessarily this will have to be done rather theoretically, with perhaps a written handout on relapse prevention supplementing your verbal explanation. You will need to do this after you have helped your client to formulate a plan which she can follow to achieve her goals after therapy has formally ended.

Spreading the effect of change. Another important way of helping to ensure that your client maintains her gains is to encourage her to practise transferring what she has learned about overcoming her problems in certain contexts to other contexts. Thus, if a client has overcome his fear of refusing unreasonable requests at work and is now asserting himself when relevant, he can take what he has learned to enable him to do this and use it to help him to say no when his parents and parents-in-law make unreasonable requests of him in his personal life. The more that clients can spread the effect of change in this way, the more they will maintain and even enhance their therapy gains.

In the following chapter, I will outline the 13 steps of the REBT treatment sequence that you need to follow in dealing with your client's problems. Understanding this sequence will help you get the most out of the transcripts of the demonstration sessions presented and analysed in Chapters 3–6.

Chapter 2
The REBT Treatment Sequence

Introduction

The REBT treatment sequence consists of 13 important steps (Figure 2.1) that are typically part of the process of helping clients to overcome their emotional problems. In particular, it illustrates the manner in which REBT's ABC model can be used as a vehicle for helping you and your client to assess and reach a common understanding of your client's problems before intervention (i.e. disputing of irrational beliefs) is attempted. The sequence further specifies the importance of teaching clients the relationship between their thoughts and feelings, the central place of homework assignments within REBT, and the desirability of helping clients to approach the goal of 'becoming their own therapists'.

The material that follows is used to demonstrate an orderly and organized implementation of the various critical components of REBT. You are advised, however, that it is not always possible (or desirable) to adhere to the framework provided by the sequence in such a neat, stepwise progression. As an example, early on in therapy a given client may appear to grasp the notion that her absolute shoulds and musts are self-defeating; subsequent sessions, however, may reveal to you that your client is actually reluctant to surrender her absolutistic demands because she regards them as a source of motivation for impelling herself to higher levels of personal achievement. When this is the case, you may have to do considerable backtracking in order to resolve this issue so that therapy will be able to proceed in an effective manner. Hence the REBT sequence is perhaps best regarded as representing a set of guidelines for the effective and efficient practice of REBT. You are cautioned against attempting to utilize these guidelines in a rigid, compulsive manner, and to watch out for your own perfectionistic demands that REBT must proceed in a tidy fashion!

Finally, it is noted that the sequence material presented in this chapter focuses on the treatment of only one particular client problem. It does not deal with issues pertaining to case management and the entire process of REBT. Such issues are discussed in Dryden and Yankura (1993).

The initial step of the sequence is presented below.

Step 1:	Ask for a problem
Step 2:	Define and agree upon the target problem (set goals in line with problem as defined)
Step 3:	Assess C
Step 4:	Assess A
Step 5:	Identify and assess any meta-emotional problems
Step 6:	Teach the iB-C connection
Step 7:	Assess iB
Step 8:	Connect iB and C
Step 9:	Dispute iB
Step 10:	Prepare your client to deepen her conviction in her rational beliefs
Step 11:	Homework: encourage your client to put her new learning into practice
Step 12:	Check homework assignments
Step 13:	Facilitate the working-through process

Steps 3 through 7 are bracketed together as: Assess the target problem (set goals in line with the problem as assessed)

Figure 2.1. The REBT treatment sequence: A= activating event (and inference); iB=irrational belief; C=emotional consequence

Step 1: Ask for a Problem

After dealing with certain practicalities (e.g. determining a fee appropriate to the client's situation), you are advised to establish a problem-solving orientation at the outset of therapy by immediately asking your client to describe the problem that she would like to discuss first. By doing so, you can indirectly communicate a number of therapeutically important messages to the client. First, quickly requesting a problem helps to emphasize that you and your client are not meeting merely to socialize and have a pleasant conversation; rather, you are going to work together to assist the client in overcoming her emotional problems. Second, it can serve to highlight the fact that REBT is a relatively efficient and focused approach to emotional problem solving. Finally, it conveys the message to your client that you are going to be quite active in the therapeutic process, and will tend to operate in such a way as to keep a problem-focused stance throughout this process.

Two main strategies: client choice versus client's most serious problem

Two basic strategies are recommended for you to utilize when attempting to elicit a target problem from a client. The first of these relies upon client choice, and involves simply asking a question, such as 'What problem would you like to work on first?' The client's response to this question may or may not be her most serious problem, but it can nevertheless provide a starting point for the therapy. The second strategy is somewhat more directive, as it involves asking the client to start with her most serious problem. Here, for example, you might ask, 'What are you most bothered about in your life right now?'

When clients fail quickly to identify a target problem

Occasionally, clients will appear to experience difficulty in identifying a target problem to focus on. When this is the case, there are a number of strategies that you can employ to encourage such clients to describe a problem area. First, you can remind your client that it is not essential to choose a serious problem to work on. It can be made clear that it is perfectly appropriate to begin the therapy process with an issue that may be impeding your client in some slight way. Here, it can be helpful to point out that there is almost always something that individuals can work on in therapy, as human beings tend to operate at a less than optimal level.

Second, you can encourage your client to identify feelings and behaviours she would like to either increase or decrease. This approach can be particularly useful for clients who are largely naive about the process of therapy, and who may be in some confusion as to just how therapy might be of help to them.

Another, less direct, means of helping your client to identify a problem area involves making an inquiry as to what she would like to accomplish from therapy. After the client has stated a particular goal, you can then ask her to describe the ways in which she is failing to achieve this goal at the present time. In many instances, such questioning can lead to fruitful discussion of self-defeating feelings and behaviours that may serve as impediments to goal attainment. You can then explore these factors with the client, without necessarily labelling them as 'problems'. Some individuals (even after they have gone to the trouble of entering therapy) have difficulty owning up to the fact that they have problems; thus, they may be discouraged from becoming engaged in a problem-focused approach such as REBT. When this appears to be the case with a particular client, you can attempt to identify and employ alternative terminology that may be more acceptable to your client.

Step 2: Define and Agree Upon the Target Problem

Frequently, the nature of your client's problem will be clear after some initial discussion during the very first session of therapy. When this is the case, you may proceed to assess the problem according to steps 3, 4 and 5 of the REBT treatment sequence. If, however, the nature of your client's problem remains unclear, it is desirable to reach an agreed definition of it prior to implementing the assessment stage. In addition, when a client discloses a number of problems in close succession, it is important to reach agreement as to which one will receive attention first.

Arriving at a common understanding of a target problem and agreeing to work on it together is an important component of REBT, as it helps to solidify the therapeutic alliance. Concurrence on these issues enables you and your client to function as a more effective team, and also helps the client to feel understood and to have confidence in your expertise. In my experience as a supervisor of REBT therapists in training, I have often reviewed audiotapes of therapy sessions in which therapist and client seemed to drift along aimlessly, in large part because the novice therapist failed to establish with the client a particular problem area on which to focus.

Distinguish between emotional and practical problems

It is useful to make a distinction with your clients between practical problems (e.g. 'I might not have enough money to pay the rent') and emotional problems (e.g. 'I'm worried to death that I might not have enough money to pay the rent') when conducting REBT. Bard (1980) has noted that REBT is an approach to therapy that is designed to assist clients in overcoming the latter type of problem; it is not designed to assist clients directly with problems falling in the former category. When clients have an emotional problem about a practical difficulty, however, this emotional problem may well become the focus of therapeutic exploration. In addition, as clients make progress in removing the emotional obstacles they create for themselves, they may experience greater success in resolving their particular practical issues (Ellis, 1985).

Target unhealthy but not healthy negative emotions

As noted in Chapter 1, irrational beliefs will tend to lead an individual to experience unhealthy negative emotional responses when faced with negative life events. Rational beliefs, on the other hand, will usually lead an individual to experience healthy (although still negative) emotional responses to these same events. Feelings such as anxiety, hurt, anger, guilt and depression are considered to stem from irrational beliefs and to represent unhealthy negative emotions, whereas feelings such as concern, disappointment, annoyance, remorse, regret and sadness are viewed as the products of rational beliefs, and regarded as healthy negative emotions.

REBT therapists do not encourage their clients to change their healthy negative emotions, as these are regarded as psychologically healthy reactions to negative events. Such emotions can motivate individuals to act on unfortunate or undesirable life circumstances in a constructive fashion, and are unlikely to impair adjustment to situations that may be largely unmodifiable. Clients *are* encouraged to change their unhealthy negative emotions, as these are more likely to stand in the way of healthy adjustment and goal attainment. In this vein, it is wise to make sure that your clients understand the distinctions between healthy and unhealthy negative emotions. Asking the question, 'How is this a problem for you?' can often lead to a useful discussion that will help you and your client to identify and define a 'real' emotional problem.

Operationalize vague problems

Clients will sometimes discuss their target problems in vague or confusing terms. When this is the case with a particular client, it is important for you to help her to operationalize the problem. This involves defining the elements of the problem in terms that will assist you in applying REBT to it.

To cite an example, a given client might state, 'My boss is a royal pain in the arse'. You can assist this client to specify the meaning of this statement by asking a question such as 'What specifically does your boss do that leads you to this conclusion, and how do you feel when he acts this way?' This type of question can help you to begin formulating the client's problem according to REBT's ABC model. The first part of the question may elicit descriptions of relevant activating events (As), while the second part may prompt the client to report on the emotional consequences (Cs) she experiences in the face of these As.

Focus on helping clients to change C, not A

Clients may often wish to focus therapy on a discussion of means to change A, rather than on their feelings (Cs) about A. Changing A constitutes a practical solution, while changing C is the emotional solution. When you encounter this situation, you can utilize certain strategies to encourage your clients to work at changing C before attempting to change A. First, you can attempt to show clients who already possess adequate practical problem-solving skills that they may be able to deploy these skills more effectively to change A if they are not emotionally disturbed at C. Second, you can attempt to show clients who lack an adequate repertoire of problem-solving skills that they will probably experience greater success in acquiring the skills needed to modify problematic As if they remove the emotional obstacles they have at C.

Dealing with failure to identify a target problem

When you have reached this stage of the assessment process and have not yet reached agreement with your client as to the nature of the problem to be targeted for change, you can recommend that the client keep a problem diary. The client would utilize this to monitor and record disturbed feelings experienced between therapy sessions with written notes concerning the types of feeling involved and when and where they were experienced.

Aim for specificity in assessing the target problem

It is important to be as specific as possible in defining and agreeing upon the target problem with clients. Clients experience emotional problems and hold related irrational beliefs in specific contexts, so that being specific will help you to obtain reliable and valid data about A, B and C. Providing clients with a sound rationale for specificity can aid this endeavour, particularly with those who tend to discuss their problems in vague terms. Clients can be taught that being specific about their target problem can help them to deal with it more constructively in the situations about which they disturb themselves. You can model specificity for clients by asking for a recent or typical example of the target problem (e.g. 'When was the last time A happened?').

In some cases, clients who remain unable to provide specific examples of their target problems may have meta-emotional problems about their primary emotional problem. When this appears to be the case, you are advised to investigate further, as in Step 5 below.

Step 3: Assess C

A and C are typically assessed prior to B. At this stage of the REBT treatment sequence you may assess either A or C, depending on which element of the target problem your client initially describes. For the purposes of this discussion, however, issues involved in the assessment of C will receive treatment first.

Re-check for an unhealthy negative emotion

In assessing C, you are advised to keep in mind that clients' emotional problems are conceptualized as unhealthy (disturbed) negative emotions, not as healthy (non-disturbed) negative emotions. Unhealthy negative emotions are targeted for change because they are strongly dysphoric, contribute to self-defeating behaviours, and block goal attainment.

Earlier in this chapter (see p. 21), I listed five healthy negative emotions and five unhealthy negative emotions. It is important to recognize, however, that your clients may not tend to employ these terms in the same way as you, an REBT therapist, do. Thus, a given client may make reference to feelings of anger when she is really experiencing annoyance, or vice versa. You should take steps to ensure that you have identified an unhealthy negative emotion, and that you are using the same terminology as the client when referring to it (Dryden, 1986b). Here, you can try to teach REBT's 'emotional vocabulary' to the client, or you may choose to adopt the client's own particular use of 'feeling language'. Regardless of the alternative chosen, it is helpful for counsellors to be consistent in their vocabulary throughout the course of treatment.

Focus on an emotional C

A client's Cs can be emotional or behavioural in nature. Dysfunctional behaviours often serve a defensive function, however, and may exist to help clients avoid experiencing certain unhealthy negative emotions. This discussion of the REBT treatment sequence, therefore, will deal with the assessment of unhealthy negative emotions rather than the assessment of dysfunctional behaviours.

Adopt the practice of attempting to identify (and treat) the unhealthy negative emotions that contribute to the dysfunctional behaviours that your clients may present. Thus, if a given client states her desire to stop smoking, you can regard smoking as a defensive behaviour and encourage your client to identify the problematic emotions she might experience if she were to refrain from it.

Clarify C

A client's unhealthy negative emotions at C can provide valuable clues concerning the nature of the irrational beliefs to which she subscribes. It is important, therefore, for you to gain clarification as to the Cs that your clients experience.

If a client is vague or unclear in attempting to describe C, there are a number of specific techniques that can be used to clarify its nature. Gestalt exercises, such as the empty-chair technique (see Passons, 1975) and Gendlin's (1978) focusing technique are sometimes helpful in this regard. In addition, imagery methods can be employed wherein the client is asked to imagine an example of her problem and to identify associated feelings that are experienced. Albert Ellis will sometimes encourage his clients to 'Take a wild guess' when they have difficulty in identifying a specific emotion; surprisingly, this method can yield useful information about C in some instances.

Frustration is an A, not a C

Clients will sometimes refer to feeling frustrated at C. Here, it is important to note that some REBT therapists prefer to regard frustration as an activating event rather than a feeling (Trexler, 1976). As a C, frustration in REBT theory is usually regarded as a healthy negative emotion that clients experience when they are blocked from attaining their goals. When a given client reports feeling frustrated, however, it is possible that she is referring to an unhealthy negative emotion. You can often determine whether a client's reported feeling of frustration is a healthy or unhealthy negative emotion by asking if the feeling is bearable or unbearable. If the client responds to such an enquiry by describing the feeling as unbearable, she may well be experiencing an unhealthy negative emotion that could be targeted for change.

Assess client motivation to change C

Clients sometimes experience unhealthy negative emotions that they are not motivated to change. This absence of motivation can occur when clients fail to recognize the destructive, self-defeating nature of the emotion in question. This situation arises most often in the case of anger; it may also occur with feelings of guilt and depression. You are therefore advised to assess clients' understanding of the dysfunctional aspects of the target emotion (C). If a particular client does not understand why her disturbed emotion is unhealthy, it is beneficial to devote as much time as necessary to helping her see this point. This can be accomplished with the following three steps:

1. Assist the client to assess the consequences of the unhealthy negative emotion. What happens when she feels this way? Does she tend to act constructively or self-defeatingly?
2. Emphasize that the goal is to replace the unhealthy negative emotion with its healthy counterpart (e.g. replacing anxiety with concern). Making this point can be difficult, particularly if the client has rigidly entrenched ideas concerning the ways she is 'supposed' to feel when confronted with negative As (see DiGiuseppe, 1984, for a more extended discussion of this issue). If provided with suitable models, however, the client will usually be able to see that she can experience the healthy emotion in a given context. To cite an example, a client with public-speaking anxiety can be helped to identify individuals she knows who experience feelings of strong concern, but not anxiety, prior to giving a lecture in front of an audience.
3. Finally, work with the client to assess the consequences that would occur if she experienced the corresponding healthy emotion when confronted with a problematic situation. As the client probably has not thought in these terms before, help her to imagine how she would behave and how the outcome might be different if she felt the healthy emotion in the face of a negative A. Then compare the outcomes of experiencing healthy versus unhealthy emotions. As an example, a given client could be encouraged to imagine how he might act (and what types of results he might get) if he felt merely annoyed (instead of angry) when his teenage son breaks his evening curfew. This may help the client to understand better the advantages of the healthy emotion, and this insight may well increase his motivation to change C.

Avoid potential pitfalls in assessing C

You may encounter a number of potential difficulties as you work to assess a client's problematic emotions at C. These difficulties may be avoided by implementing the following suggestions:

1. Avoid using questions that reinforce the notion that A causes C. You may make the error of asking clients questions such as 'How does the situation make you feel?' As an alternative, you might ask 'How do you feel about the situation?' This question can serve to elicit

descriptions of problematic Cs, and does not implicitly convey the message that A causes C.

2. When clients respond to enquiries concerning their feelings about A with terms such as 'bad', upset', 'miserable', etc., do not attempt to work with these vague descriptions of emotions. Instead, work with clients to help them clarify exactly what feelings they experience at C. Also, do not accept statements such as 'I feel trapped' or 'I felt rejected' as descriptions of emotions occurring at C. Trapped and rejected are not emotions. These terms probably refer to combinations of A, B and C factors, and it is important to discriminate between these three and ensure that clients' C statements really do refer to feelings. To illustrate, if a client states 'I felt rejected', she can be helped to see that rejection is an A and then asked how she felt about the rejection at point C (e.g. hurt, ashamed, etc.).

Step 4: Assess A

If C is assessed first, the next step in the REBT treatment sequence is to assess A. A can refer to activating events that may be regarded as a confirmable reality (i.e. neutral observers could confirm a given client's descriptions of A). In this presentation, however, A will also be used to stand for clients' inferences about the activating event.

As with assessments of C, aim for specificity when assessing A. This can be accomplished by asking the client to provide the most recent occurrence of A, a typical example of A, or the most relevant example the client can recall.

Identify the critical A

In the process of assessing A, it is important to help the client to identify the critical A (i.e. the part that generally serves to trigger irrational beliefs at B). Identifying this trigger can sometimes be complicated by inferences that the client makes about the situation. As these inferences are often linked (or chained) together, the technique referred to as inference chaining (described fully in Dryden, 1995a) can be used to identify the particular inference in the chain that functions as the trigger.

By way of illustration, imagine a client who experiences anxiety at point C. Initial inquiry reveals that she is due to give a class presentation. Giving the class presentation thus represents an activating event, but you will wish to determine just what it is about the presentation that is anxiety-provoking in the client's mind. The following dialogue might then ensue:

You:	What aspect of giving the presentation are you anxious about?
Client:	Well, I'm afraid I may not do a very good job.
You:	For the moment, let's assume that you don't. What's anxiety-provoking in your mind about that?
Client:	Well, if I don't do a good job in class, then my teacher will give me a poor grade.
You:	Let's assume that as well. What would you be anxious about there?
Client:	That I might flunk the course.
You:	And if you did?
Client:	Oh, my God, I couldn't face my father!
You:	Imagine telling your father that you had failed. What would be anxiety-provoking about that in your mind?
Client:	I can just picture his reaction — he would be devastated!
You:	And how would you feel if that happened?
Client:	Oh God, that would be terrible! I really couldn't stand to see my father cry — I'd feel so very sorry for him!

The class presentation was initially identified as A by the client. Through inference chaining, however, you have discovered the client's fearful anticipation of her father's upset upon hearing of her presumed failure.

To test whether a given inference in a chain genuinely represents the client's critical, you might write down the inference chain, review it with the client, and ask her to identify the point that she thinks is the most important. Another technique for confirming whether or not the newly identified aspect of A is critical is to 'manipulate' A and then check the client's responses at C. Thus, for example, you could say to the client, 'Let's suppose you told your father that you failed the course, and he wasn't devastated — in fact, he coped quite well with the news. Would that different turn of events have any impact on your anxiety about giving the class presentation?' If the client responds in the affirmative, you can be more confident that the problem has been accurately assessed. If the client indicates that she would still be anxious, this could indicate that the prospect of seeing her father cry (at A) is not the most relevant factor in her anxiety problem.

Once the critical A has been established, it is important to reassess any changes in the client's feelings at C since the initial analysis of the problem. Assuming that the new aspect of A revealed in the above illustration is indeed the central factor, it would be important to encourage the client to see that her anxiety is more closely associated with the overwhelming pity for her father she would feel at C, than with any general fears of failure she might have. Two alternative courses then present themselves in terms of treatment: the first would involve focusing on the client's feelings of anxiety at C about the future prospect of her father's emotional devastation. The second would involve asking the client to assume that the new A (the father's upset) had already occurred, and then dealing with the feelings of other pity that would presumably occur at C.

A can refer to many things

REBT therapists generally agree that A can be a thought, an inference, an image, a sensation, or a behaviour, as well as an actual event in the client's environment that can be confirmed by neutral observers. In addition, a client's feelings at C may also serve as an A. A given client may, for example, experience guilt feelings at C. This guilt could then serve as a new A, and the client may feel ashamed (a new C) about feeling guilty. Here, the client has a meta-emotional problem about an original emotional problem. Not all clients will present such meta-problems, but the process of determining whether or not they exist is an important part of assessment in the REBT treatment sequence (see Step 5).

Assume (at least temporarily) that A is true

In the course of assessing A, it will sometimes become apparent to you that your client's critical A is a clear distortion of reality. When this is the case, it can be tempting to dispute A in order to correct the client's faulty inferences.

Generally, you are advised to resist this temptation and to encourage your client to temporarily assume that A is correct. In the case previously described, for example, it is not essential to determine whether or not the client's father would truly be devastated upon hearing about her failure. Rather, it is important to treat A as if it is an accurate depiction of reality, in order to assist the client in identifying the irrational beliefs that are at the core of her particular feelings at C.

Avoid pitfalls in assessing A

A number of potential pitfalls that you may encounter in assessing A may be avoided by implementing the following suggestions:

1. Refrain from obtaining too much detail about A. Allowing clients to speak at length about A can turn therapy into a gripe session, which will make it difficult to maintain a problem-solving approach to overcoming emotional difficulties. With clients who tend to ramble or provide compulsive details concerning their As, you can attempt to abstract the most salient theme, or what appears to be the major aspect of A. At times, it is appropriate tactfully to interrupt clients in

order to re-establish a specific focus. You might say, for instance, 'I think you may be providing me with more detail than I require. Can you tell me what it was about the situation that upset you most?'

2. Discourage clients from describing A in vague terms. Attempt to obtain as clear and specific an example of A as possible. An example of a vague A would be, 'My husband was really on my case last night.' In contrast, a specific A would be, 'My husband told me I was lazy and inept for not having dinner ready and waiting for him when he arrived from work.'

3. Discourage clients from talking about several As at one time. Some individuals will jump from event to event within a given counselling session; in REBT, it is important to work on one A at a time. Clients can be encouraged to deal with the A they consider to best illustrate the context within which they make themselves disturbed, and can be assured that their other As can be dealt with later on.

4. If at this point of the sequence a given client still has not identified a clear A, encourage her to start a diary prior to the next session. This diary can be used to record examples of activating events about which she makes herself disturbed.

Agree on Goals

It has been emphasized that it is important for you and your client to develop a common understanding of your client's target problem. Likewise, it is desirable to reach agreement as to the client's goals for change, as this will facilitate the development of a sound therapeutic alliance between the two of you.

When to agree on goals

There are two main points at which you will want to assess a given client's goals for change. The first point occurs when you and your client have defined and reached agreement concerning the client's target problem (Step 2). Here, it is recommended that you help your client to set a goal in line with the problem as initially assessed. Thus, if a particular client's problem relates to being overweight, an initial goal would be for her to achieve and maintain a specific target weight.

You may, however, wish to reconsider and reformulate the client's goal at the assessment stage (Steps 3, 4 and 5). For example, after agreeing that the client's goal is to achieve and maintain a specific weight, assessment may reveal that she becomes anxious and overeats when she is bored. At this point, the client's goal might be reformulated so that it focuses on her ability to deal more appropriately with boredom, so that she less often resorts to the (self-defeating) coping strategy of overeating. The client can be encouraged to work at feeling con-cerned (rather than anxious) about being bored, and to use that feeling of concern to deal with boredom in more constructive ways. Generally, it is helpful to encourage clients to select a healthy negative emotion as a goal, and to assist them in understanding why such an emotion repre-sents a realistic and constructive response to a negative activating event at A.

Help clients take a long-term perspective

When discussing goals with clients, it is useful to make them cognizant of the distinction between long-term goals and short-term goals. At times, clients may wish to settle on a short-term goal that may in the long term be self-defeating and therefore irrational (e.g. in the case of a client who shoplifts, the desire to steal without experiencing guilt feel-ings). You are advised to help clients adopt a broader perspective and to obtain their commitment to work towards productive long-term goals.

Avoid pitfalls when agreeing on goals

Several potential difficulties may be encountered when working with clients to establish goals. The following suggestions may prove helpful in avoiding them.

1. Do not accept clients' goal statements when they express a desire to experience less of an unhealthy negative emotion (e.g. 'I wanted to feel less anxious', or 'I want to feel less guilty'). REBT theory main-tains that the presence of an unhealthy negative emotion (such as anxiety or guilt) indicates that the client experiencing that emotion is subscribing to an irrational belief. As such, it is advisable to help clients to distinguish between the unhealthy negative emotion in question and its healthy counterpart. Clients can be encouraged to set the latter type of emotion as their goal. They can work, therefore, at feeling concerned instead of anxious, or sorry rather than guilty and self-downing.

2. Do not accept client goals that express the wish to feel neutral, indif-ferent or calm with respect to events about which it would be ratio-nal to experience a healthy negative emotion. Emotions indicating indifference (e.g. calmness in the face of an unfortunate event) would mean that a given client did not have a rational belief about the event in question, whereas in reality the client would probably prefer that the event not occur. Acquiescing to the client's goal to feel calm or indifferent about a negative event may actually encour-age her to deny the existence of her desires, rather than to think rationally.

3. For similar reasons, do not accept client goals that involve experiencing positive feelings about a negative A. It would be unrealistic for an individual to feel happy about a negative life event she would prefer not to encounter. Accepting the goal of feeling positive about a negative event may encourage clients to believe that it is good that a particular negative A occurred. This is undesirable, as it fails to promote rational thinking. To reiterate an earlier point, clients who become better able to experience a healthy (as opposed to unhealthy) negative feeling in the face of a negative life event may be more psychologically prepared to either accept it or modify it.

4. Do not accept vague goals, such as 'I want to be happy.' The more specific you can encourage your client to be in setting goals, the more likely it is that she will be motivated to do the hard work of changing her irrational beliefs in the service of achieving these goals.

5. Finally, do not set goals that are not within your client's direct control. You cannot, for example, help any client to change another person because this is not in her direct control. You can help her to put into practice strategies that *may* have the outcome of influencing the other to change. These strategies, as they are enacted by the client, are within her control

Step 5: Identify and Assess any Meta-Emotional Problems

Clients can frequently have meta-emotional problems about their primary emotional problem. If a particular client's primary problem is anxiety, for instance, you can check for the presence of a meta-emotional problem (such as shame about feeling anxious) by asking a question such as, 'How do you feel about feeling anxious?'

When to attend to the meta-emotional problem first

It is suggested that you attend to the client's meta-problem if any of the following conditions are met:

1. The client's meta-problem significantly interferes with the work being done on her primary problem.
2. From a clinical perspective, the meta-problem appears to be the more important of the two.
3. The client can see the sense of working on her meta-emotional problem first.

It can be important to present clients with a plausible rationale for working on the meta-problem first. If the client still wishes to work on the primary problem first, even after a reasonable explanation has been provided, then it is advisable to do so. To do otherwise could jeopardize the therapeutic alliance between you.

Check for an emotional problem about a healthy negative emotion

In the course of assessing a client's stated primary problem, it may become evident that she is in fact experiencing a healthy negative emotion (e.g. sadness in the face of an important loss). If this is the case, check to see whether your client has a problem with this healthy emotion. A client may, for example, feel ashamed about feeling sad. Work to reach agreement that the meta-emotional problem (shame) will be the client's target problem and proceed to assess the agreed-upon problem.

Assess for the presence of shame

As noted above, clients who are reluctant to disclose an emotional problem may feel ashamed about having the problem, or about admitting it to a therapist. You can attempt to surmount this difficulty by asking such clients how they would feel if they did have an emotional problem about the activating event under discussion. With clients who provide indications that they would feel ashamed, you can attempt to reach agreement to work on shame as the target problem before encouraging disclosure of the original problem.

Step 6: Teach the iB-C Connection

By this stage, the A and C elements of a client's primary or meta-emotional problem have been assessed. The next step is for you to teach the client the iB-C connection, that is, the concept that at the core of emotional problems lie irrational beliefs and that these problems are not determined by activating events. This is best done by teaching your client the general principle that irrational beliefs are at a core of emotional disturbance. You will have an opportunity to connect your client's specific irrational beliefs with her unhealthy negative emotion in Step 8. This step is critical, because unless the client understands that irrational beliefs are at the core of emotional problems, she will not understand why these beliefs will be assessed during the next step of the treatment process. Utilizing an example unrelated to the client's problem can often be helpful in explaining this concept. A number of exercises and metaphors for conveying this idea are described in Dryden (1995a).

Step 7: Assess Irrational Beliefs

In assessing irrational beliefs it is important for you (1) to keep in mind the distinction between your clients' rational and irrational beliefs, and (2) to help them to understand the differences between these two types of thinking.

Assessing both premise and derivative forms of irrational beliefs

In Chapter 1, I introduced you to the differences between rational and irrational beliefs and noted that irrational beliefs are often composed of a premise and certain derivatives that tend to stem from that premise. To briefly review, the premise component of irrational beliefs embodies absolutistic shoulds, musts, have tos, etc.; these can be expressed as demands directed at self, others, or the world and life conditions. The three main irrational derivatives are awfulizing, low frustration tolerance and damnation.

At this stage of the REBT treatment sequence, you will want to assess carefully both the premise and the derivative components of your client's irrational beliefs. With respect to irrational derivatives, you may either teach and use the REBT terms for these processes, or use your client's own language. If the latter alternative is chosen, however, it is advisable to make sure that the terms used by your client accurately reflect irrational beliefs. This decision can be based on client feedback concerning the strategy perceived to be most helpful.

Distinguish between absolute shoulds and other shoulds

You can become highly attuned to indications that your clients are harbouring particular irrational beliefs in their thinking. It is important to bear in mind, however, that every client utterance of the word 'should' does not constitute evidence for the presence of an irrational belief. Most expressions of the word should, in fact, will be unrelated to a given client's emotional problems, as this word has multiple meanings in the English language. These include shoulds of preference (e.g. 'I should get to work on time'); empirical or probabilistic shoulds (e.g. 'When two parts of hydrogen and one part of oxygen are combined, you should get water'); and shoulds of recommendation (e.g. 'You should see the new Disney movie').

REBT theory hypothesizes that only absolute shoulds are related to emotional disturbance. When clients find the different meanings confusing, it can sometimes be useful to substitute the word must in cases where an irrational belief in its premise form may be operative (compare, for instance, 'I should be admired by my colleagues' and 'I must be admired by my colleagues'). Clinical experience suggests that the word must conveys the meaning of absolute demandingness better than the word should. In particular, clients can be helped to distinguish between absolute shoulds and shoulds of preference.

Use questions to assess irrational beliefs

You are advised to employ questions when assessing your clients' irrational beliefs. An example of a standard question used by REBT therapists is 'What were you telling yourself about A to make yourself disturbed at C?' This type of open-ended question offers both advantages and disadvantages.

One advantage of such a question is that it embodies and may convey several important elements of the REBT theory of emotional disturbance. In essence, it reinforces in the client the concept that A does not cause C: it is iB that largely determines whether healthy or unhealthy negative emotions are experienced at C. An additional advantage of the above type of enquiry is that it is unlikely to put words in the client's mouth concerning the content of her beliefs.

The main disadvantage of using this type of question is that clients (particularly those who are new to REBT) will frequently not respond to it by articulating an irrational belief. Instead, they may respond by providing further inferences about A — and, in some cases, these inferences may well be less relevant than the one previously selected at Step 4.

Imagine, for example, that a given client is particularly anxious that other people will think she is a fool if she stammers in public. If you ask, 'What were you telling yourself about other people's criticism to make yourself anxious at C?', she may conceivably respond by stating 'I thought they wouldn't like me.' Note that this response is actually an inference about A, and that it fails to reveal the client's irrational belief. Here, you would try to help the client see that her statement does not describe an irrational belief, and then educate her to look further for her anxiety-provoking irrational belief about A. This can be done by judiciously combining the use of open-ended questions with didactic explanation.

Walen, DiGiuseppe and Dryden (1992) list a number of other open-ended questions that may be used to assess clients' irrational beliefs. These include: 'What was going through your mind?'; 'Were you aware of any thoughts in your head?'; 'What was on your mind then?' and 'Are you aware of what you were thinking at that moment?' Again, clients will not necessarily disclose irrational beliefs in response to these questions; they may require further help of a didactic nature.

Theory-driven questions represent an alternative to the use of open-ended questions for assessing irrational beliefs. Such questions are derived directly from REBT theory, and are more specific with respect to identifying the type of response that is desired. As an example, attempting to elicit a response concerning a client's operative must (i.e. a premise), you might ask, 'What demand were you making about other people's criticism to make yourself disturbed at point C?' By way of further illustration, the following question could be used to assess for a particular derivative of an irrational premise: 'What kind of person did you think you were for stammering and incurring other people's criticism?'

Theory-driven questions are useful in so far as they orient the client to look for her irrational beliefs. In using them, however, you run the risk of putting words into the client's mouth and encouraging her to look for irrational beliefs that she may not actually hold. This risk is minimized when careful assessment has already established that the client has an unhealthy negative emotion at point C.

Step 8: Connect Irrational Beliefs and C

After assessing your client's irrational beliefs in both premise and derivative form, you should take care to ensure that she grasps the connection between her irrational beliefs and her disturbed emotions at point C. This step should precede any attempts at disputing these beliefs.

A simple enquiry can be used to determine whether your client understands this very important connection. Thus, you might say, 'Can you understand that as long as you demand that other people must not criticize you, you are bound to make yourself anxious about the possibility that this might occur?' With respect to an irrational derivative, you may ask, 'Can you see that as long as you believe that you are no good for being regarded by others as a fool, you will be anxious about being criticized?' If the client responds in the affirmative, you can then attempt to elicit from the client the iB-C connection: 'So, in order to change your feeling of anxiety to one of concern, what do you need to change first?' Eliciting this connection is likely to be more productive than simply telling the client that such a connection exists. If the client fails to see the connection, spend time helping her to understand it before proceeding to dispute her irrational beliefs.

Step 9: Dispute Irrational Beliefs

After conducting a thorough assessment of the target problem, identifying and assessing any meta-emotional problems, and teaching the iB-C connection, the next step in the REBT treatment sequence is to begin the process of disputing clients' irrational beliefs.

The goals of disputing

A major goal of disputing at this point is to help clients to understand that the irrational beliefs to which they subscribe are unproductive (in the sense that they lead to self-defeating emotions and behaviours), illogical and inconsistent with reality and that the alternatives to these beliefs (i.e. rational beliefs) are productive, logical and consistent with reality.

Even if a given client provides evidence that she has reached such an understanding, it would probably be an error for you to assume that her conviction in the alternative rational belief will be strong. In this vein, it can be helpful to teach the client the distinction between light conviction and deep conviction in a rational belief. The former state is considered characteristic of intellectual rational insight, while the latter state is characteristic of emotional rational insight. Clients can be encouraged to view even a light conviction in an alternative rational belief as a sign of progress, albeit usually insufficient in itself to promote emotional change.

With specific regard to the target problem, the goals of disputing are to help the client to understand the following:

1. *Musts*: human beings quite frequently change their preferences to absolute demands (i.e. irrational beliefs). It is very likely that there is no evidence in support of the absolute demands embodied in irrational beliefs, whereas evidence can be found to support preferences.
2. *Awfulizing*: individuals experiencing emotional disturbance are often defining their negative As as being absolutely awful (i.e. 101 per cent bad). This constitutes magical nonsense, for in reality all experience lies within a 0–99.99 per cent range of badness.
3. *Low Frustration Tolerance*: human beings can virtually always tolerate and survive that which they think they cannot stand, and can find some degree of happiness even if their negative As persist.
4. *Damnation*: this is a concept that is illogical and inconsistent with reality and will lead to emotional trouble. The preferable alternative to damnation is for human beings to accept themselves, other people and the world as imperfect and complex — too complex to be given a single global rating.

As therapy proceeds, you can pursue the goal of helping clients to internalize a broad range of rational beliefs so that they become part of a general philosophy of rational living. This process, however, is beyond the scope of this book.

Use questions during disputing

In the first stage of the disputing sequence, you can ask clients to provide evidence in support of their musts. Some standard questions used for this purpose include, 'Where is the evidence that you must under all conditions...?'; 'Where is the proof that you must...?'; 'Is it true that you absolutely must...?'; and 'Where is it written that you must...?'

It is important to ensure that clients actually answer the disputing questions asked of them. For example, in response to the question 'Why must you succeed?' a given client might answer, 'Because succeeding will bring me certain advantages.' Note that the client has really not addressed herself to the question that was asked; rather, she has actually provided a response to the question, 'Why is it preferable for you to succeed?' Generally, it is good practice to anticipate that clients will not immediately provide correct responses to initial disputing questions.

According to REBT theory, the only valid answer to the question 'Why must you succeed?' is 'There is no reason why I absolutely must, although it would be preferable.' When clients provide any other answer, it is likely that they need to be educated as to why their answer is (1) incorrect with respect to the question that was asked, or (2) a correct answer to a different question. During this process a combination of questions and short didactic explanations may be used to help clients attain an understanding of the correct answer.

It is usually helpful at this point to assist clients in distinguishing between their rational and irrational beliefs. One means for accomplishing this is to write down two questions, such as the following:

1. Why must you succeed?
2. Why is it preferable, but not essential for you to succeed?

When clients attempt to answer these questions, it is often the case that they will give the same answer to both. When this occurs, they can be helped to see that the reasons they provided in their response constitute evidence for their rational belief, but not for their irrational belief. Here, the goal is to help clients to comprehend that the only answer to a question concerning the existence of musts is — to paraphrase Ellis — 'There are in all probability no absolute musts in the universe.'

Persistence in disputing

As noted earlier, it is important to dispute both the premise and the derivative forms of a given client's irrational beliefs. If, however, you have started this process by disputing the irrational premise, it is important to persist in this endeavour until your client is able to see that there is no evidence in support of this premise before beginning to dispute a derivative from the premise.

Switching too quickly from premise to derivative (and vice versa) during disputing can be confusing for the client. If, however, disputing is initially aimed at an irrational premise and it becomes clear that the client is not finding this helpful, it can make sense to redirect the focus toward a derivative and monitor the client's reactions. Some clients appear to have an easier time understanding why their derivatives are irrational than why their musts are irrational.

Use a variety of disputing strategies

There are three main foci for disputing irrational beliefs. It is probably preferable to use all three of these strategies whenever possible.

1. *Focus on illogicality*: here, clients are helped to understand why their irrational beliefs are illogical. They are shown, for instance, that simply because they may want something to happen, it does not logically follow that it absolutely must happen. You can show clients that their irrational beliefs often represent illogical *non sequiturs*.

2. *Focus on empiricism*: the goal of this strategy is to demonstrate to clients that their musts and irrational derivatives are almost always inconsistent with reality. To accomplish this goal, use questions that ask clients to provide evidence in support of their irrational beliefs (e.g. 'Where is the evidence that you must succeed?'). A given client could be helped to see that if there was evidence to support her belief that she must succeed, then she would have to succeed no matter what she believed. If she is not succeeding at present, that fact constitutes evidence that her irrational belief is empirically inconsistent with reality.

3. *Focus on pragmatism*: with this strategy, focus on showing clients the pragmatic consequences of holding irrational beliefs. The goal is to help clients see that as long as they subscribe to their irrational musts and their derivatives, they will remain disturbed. Here, questions such as, 'What is believing that you must succeed going to get you other than anxious and depressed?' are used.

After disputing an irrational belief, clients need to learn how to replace their irrational belief with a new, rational belief. So work together with your clients to construct a rational belief that appears to be most adaptive with respect to A. After an alternative rational belief has been formulated, the three disputing strategies described above can be applied to it in order to demonstrate to clients that rational beliefs are in fact rational. It is much better for your clients to see for themselves the evidence that rational beliefs are more valid and helpful, than for you to tell them simply that this is so.

Use a variety of disputing styles

While seasoned practitioners of REBT tend to develop their own individual disputing styles, four basic styles for disputing irrational beliefs
will be emphasized here. These four styles are termed Socratic, didactic,
humorous and self-disclosing.

Socratic style

When utilizing the Socratic style of disputing, you set yourself the task
of asking clients questions concerning the illogical, empirically inconsistent and dysfunctional aspects of their irrational beliefs. Such questions
are intended to prompt clients to think for themselves, as opposed to
simply accepting the counsellor's viewpoint because it stems from a
background of expertise. Although the Socratic style emphasizes the
use of questions, it can be supplemented with brief explanations
designed to correct quickly client misconceptions that may arise along
the way.

Didactic style

Although a good number of REBT therapists seem to prefer using the
Socratic style, it is acknowledged that the use of questions does not
always prove productive. When this is the case, you can shift to utilizing
brief, direct, didactic explanations as to why irrational beliefs are self-
defeating and rational beliefs are more productive. It is quite likely that
almost all counsellors find it helpful to use didactic explanations at various points in the treatment process.

When didactic explanations are employed, it is good practice to
check whether clients have understood the message conveyed. One
means of doing this is to request that they paraphrase the points made.
Here, you might make a statement such as, 'I'm not quite sure I'm making myself clear to you — perhaps you could put into your own words
what you think I've been saying to you.' It can be a mistake to accept
clients' non-verbal and paraverbal signs of understanding (e.g. head
nods, mm-hmms) without questioning them. Clients will sometimes
evince understanding even when they actually have not understood a
word you have said (Dryden, 1986b).

Humorous style

With some clients, the use of humour or humorous exaggeration can
represent a productive vehicle for making the point that there is no evidence to support irrational beliefs. The use of humour as a disputing
strategy, however, is advised only when the following conditions are

met: (1) you have established a good working relationship with the client; (2) the client has already provided some evidence that she has a good sense of humour; and (3) the humorous interventions are directed at the irrationality of the client's belief and not at the client as a person. In addition, Ellis (1985) has noted that it is important for REBT therapists to refrain from overusing techniques that they find enjoyable at clients' expense.

Self-disclosing style

Counsellor self-disclosure can represent another useful means of disputing clients' irrational beliefs. Generally, the coping model (as opposed to the mastery model) of self-disclosure is viewed as having features that are likely to be helpful to clients. By using the coping model, you reveal that: (1) you have experienced a problem that in some sense is similar to your client's problem; (2) you once held an irrational belief that is similar to the one the client maintains; and (3) you worked at changing this belief and thus no longer have the problem.

In contrast to the coping model of self-disclosure, the mastery model would involve telling the client that you have never experienced a problem similar to the client's because you have always thought rationally about the issue at hand. Although this approach can highlight the fact that rational thinking helps an individual to avoid particular emotional problems, it can be disadvantageous in so far as it accentuates the differences between you and your client. In my experience, the mastery model is less productive than the coping model in encouraging clients to challenge their irrationality. I would note, however, that some clients will not even find the coping model useful. Particular clients, for instance, will tend to condemn you when you display any signs of 'weakness'. If it becomes apparent that attempts at self-disclosure are failing to benefit the client (and are perhaps damaging the therapeutic alliance), other disputing strategies may be used instead.

Step 10: Prepare Clients to Deepen Their Conviction in Rational Beliefs

Once your clients have acknowledged that (1) there is no evidence in support of irrational beliefs, but rational beliefs can be supported by evidence; (2) it is more logical to think rationally; and (3) rational beliefs will lead to more productive emotional results than irrational beliefs, you are in a position to help them deepen their conviction in their new, alternative rational beliefs.

Emphasize that weak conviction in a rational belief is unlikely (on its own) to promote change

Intellectual rational insight is usually insufficient to bring about meaningful and behavioural change. As such, at this stage of the REBT sequence, help your clients to see that weak conviction in rational beliefs — although important — is unlikely to help them reach their therapy goals. This can be accomplished with brief discussion of the REBT view of therapeutic change. Through the use of Socratic questioning and brief didactic explanations (as per Step 9), clients can be helped to understand that they will strengthen their conviction in their new rational beliefs by disputing irrational beliefs (and replacing them with their rational alternatives) within and between therapy sessions. Clients should also understand that this process will require them to act against their irrational beliefs as well as to dispute them cognitively. Teaching this concept now will make it easier for you to encourage clients to put their new learning into practice (Steps 11 and 12) and to facilitate the working-through process (Step 13).

Dealing with the 'head–gut' issue

As clients learn to think more rationally, they may sometimes make statements such as, 'I understand that my rational belief will help me to achieve my goals, but I don't really believe in it yet.' You can anticipate that clients will often experience some difficulty in crossing the bridge between intellectual and emotional insight, and can initiate discussion on this point as a prelude to consideration of ways to deepen conviction in rational beliefs and weaken conviction in irrational ones. As an example, you might ask a client, 'What do you think you'll have to do in order to get your new rational belief into your gut?'

It is good practice to encourage clients to commit themselves to a process of therapeutic change that will require repeated and forceful disputing of irrational beliefs, as well as efforts to practise rational thinking within relevant life contexts. Here, clients are helped to design and undertake a variety of homework assignments, as described in Step 11.

Step 11: Encouraging Clients to Put New Learning into Practice

At this point, clients should be ready to put their rational beliefs into practice. They can be reminded that, according to the REBT theory of therapeutic change, they will have greater success in deepening conviction in their rational beliefs if they work at disputing irrational beliefs and strengthening rational ones in situations that are the same or similar to the activating event previously assessed. REBT advocates a variety of homework assignments for accomplishing this end and these assignments can be categorized according to whether they have a cognitive, behavioural or imagery focus. In using homework assignments with clients, you should bear in mind the following important points:

1. *Ensure that homework assignments are relevant.* You are advised to develop homework activities that are relevant to the irrational belief targeted for change. Enacting the homework assignment will help the client to weaken conviction in this irrational belief and deepen conviction in the alternative rational belief.

2. *Collaborate with clients.* It is good practice to enlist clients' active collaboration when discussing appropriate homework assignments. In order to increase the likelihood that a particular assignment will be enacted, you should ensure that your client (1) sees the sense of doing the homework assignment; (2) agrees that carrying out the assignment will help in the attainment of desired goals; and (3) has some degree of confidence in her ability to carry out the assignment. The probability of client compliance with homework assignments can be further maximized by establishing when, where and how often the particular activity will be implemented.

3. *Be prepared to compromise.* Ideally, homework assignments involve having clients actively and forcefully dispute their irrational beliefs in the most relevant life contexts possible. If, however, this is not feasible, clients can be encouraged to (1) dispute their irrational beliefs in situations that approximate the most relevant A, or (2) use imagery to dispute irrational beliefs while vividly imagining A. Doing these less-than-ideal assignments can sometimes increase the likelihood that clients will eventually take on more challenging homework activities (Ellis, 1983).

4. *Assess and troubleshoot obstacles.* You can work with your clients to specify in advance any obstacles that may serve as impediments to homework completion. Clients can be encouraged to find possible ways of overcoming these obstacles before carrying out the assignment.

5. *Use homework at different times during therapy.* The present discussion has focused on homework assignments that help clients to strengthen conviction in their rational beliefs. It should be noted, however, that homework assignments can be useful at various points and for various purposes throughout the treatment sequence. Thus, homework assignments can be designed to help clients (1) specify their problematic emotions at C; (2) detect their irrational beliefs at B; and (3) identify the most relevant aspect of A about which they have made themselves disturbed. In addition, homework assign-

ments can also be used as a means for educating clients about the ABCs of REBT. Clients can be encouraged to read particular books (bibliotherapy), or to listen to REBT lectures on audiotape. When suggesting such assignments, it is wise to select material that is relevant to the target problem and readily understandable. You can consider creating your own written materials or audiotapes to use with particular clients when appropriate material is not available. Because the two teaching transcripts presented in Chapters 3 and 5 are of single demonstration sessions, they cannot illustrate the use of homework assignments across the process of therapy. For the same reason, these transcripts do not illustrate the final two steps in the treatment sequence, which will be discussed for the sake of completion.

Step 12: Check Homework Assignments

It is good practice to review previously negotiated homework assignments at the start of each session. Failure to do so may inadvertently communicate to clients that you do not consider these assignments to be an integral part of the change process. This is undesirable, as homework assignments are central to helping clients achieve their therapy goals.

Confirm that clients faced A

Unfortunately, clients can be quite creative in developing strategies to avoid problematic As. It is advisable for you to ascertain that your clients actually faced the As they committed themselves to confronting. When clients genuinely have faced their As, they typically report that they first made themselves disturbed and then managed to become undisturbed (without simply escaping from the situation) by utilizing the disputing techniques discussed in counselling. When clients fail to carry out their homework assignments in this manner, you can help them to identify and deal with any obstacles that may have been involved. You can then encourage your clients to again confront their troublesome situations and use vigorous disputing to make themselves undisturbed within that context. As necessary, appropriate disputes can be modelled and rehearsed in the session before clients make another attempt to confront the A in question.

Verify that clients changed iB

When clients report success in implementing homework assignments, it is good practice to determine whether this success can be attributed to

(1) changing an irrational belief to its rational alternative; (2) changing either A itself or inferences about A; or (3) the use of distraction techniques. If enquiry reveals that a given client utilized the last two methods, you can acknowledge the client's efforts but then point out that these strategies may not be helpful in the long term. Practical solutions (i.e. changing A) or distractions are merely palliative, as they do not require clients to change the irrational beliefs that produce unhealthy negative emotions when A is faced. Many As are unavoidable; the emotional problem will tend to reassert itself again and again. You can attempt to convey these points to clients, encourage them to again face the situation at A, and elicit their commitment to dispute their irrational beliefs and practise acting on the basis of the new rational beliefs.

Deal with failure to complete homework assignments

When clients fail to execute agreed-on homework, accept them as fallible human beings and help them to identify the reasons why the assignment was not carried out. The ABC framework can be used to help clients identify possible irrational beliefs that interfered with homework completion. In particular, you will want to assess for irrational beliefs that contribute to low frustration tolerance (e.g. 'I shouldn't have to work so hard at changing — it's too damn hard!'). When clients hold such beliefs, they can be helped to challenge and change them prior to reassignment of the homework.

Step 13: Facilitate the Working-through Process

It is unlikely that clients will achieve enduring therapeutic change unless they repeatedly and forcefully challenge their irrational beliefs in relevant contexts at A. By engaging in this process, they will further strengthen their conviction in rational beliefs and continue to weaken their conviction in irrational ones. The working-through process represents a means by which clients integrate rational beliefs into their emotional and behavioural repertoires.

Suggest a variety of homework assignments targeted at the same irrational belief

When clients have experienced some success in disputing particular irrational beliefs irrelevant situations at A, they can be encouraged to use different types of homework activities to further erode the degree to which they subscribe to these same beliefs. Doing so teaches clients that a variety of methods can be used to dispute their targeted irrational beliefs, as well as others. In addition, introducing this sort of variety can help to sustain clients' interest in the change process.

Discuss the non-linear model of change

You can explain that change is a non-linear process in order to prepare clients for the difficulties they may encounter as they try to dispute irrational beliefs within a wide variety of contexts. Potential setbacks can be identified, and clients can be helped in advance to develop ways of dealing with them. Specifically, clients can be given assistance in identifying and challenging the irrational beliefs that might underpin their relapses.

In addition, you can teach clients to evaluate change on the following three major dimensions:

1. *Frequency*: are unhealthy negative emotions experienced less often than before?
2. *Intensity*: when unhealthy negative emotions are experienced, are they less intense than before?
3. *Duration*: do unhealthy emotional episodes last for shorter periods than before?

Clients can be encouraged to keep records of their disturbed emotions at point C, using these three criteria for change. In addition, clients may find it helpful to read the booklet, *How to Maintain and Enhance Your Rational-Emotive Therapy Gains* (Ellis, 1984). This publication contains many useful suggestions that clients may use to facilitate the working-through process and is reproduced in Dryden and Yankura (1993).

Encourage clients to take responsibility for continued progress

At this stage, clients can be helped to develop their own homework assignments to change their target beliefs and to change other irrational beliefs in different situations. If, for example, a given client has been successful in disputing an irrational belief about approval in a work-related situation that involves criticism, she might be encouraged to dispute this belief in other situations in which criticism is encountered (e.g. with family members or friends). As clients develop confidence in designing and carrying out their own homework assignments, they are likely to experience increasing success in acting as their own therapists. This accomplishment is most important, as the long-term goal of REBT is to encourage clients to internalize the REBT model of change and to take responsibility for further progress after therapy has ended.

The rest of this book is devoted to the analysis of verbatim teaching transcripts of REBT demonstration sessions. I will refer to the REBT treatment sequence in commenting on these transcripts. As such, it is important that you thoroughly familiarize yourself with Steps 1–11 of this sequence. Take time to study and re-read this chapter several times before proceeding to the following chapters.

Chapter 3
Transcript of Demonstration Session I. Therapist: Windy Dryden

There are basically two ways of conducting a live demonstration session of REBT in the context of an introductory REBT training workshop. First, the course organizer can arrange for volunteers from outside the training course to discuss a personal problem with the trainer in front of the training cohort. Second, the trainer can call for volunteers from among the trainees themselves to discuss a personal problem with the trainer who serves as therapist. In this chapter, I present a transcript of the former while in Chapter 5, I present a transcript of the latter.

When the course organizer arranges for a volunteer from outside the course to take part in a demonstration session of REBT, the following safeguards need to be in place:

1. The course organizer needs to explain the purpose of the demonstration session to the volunteer — it is to help trainees to learn more about the therapy approach that they are learning by seeing it in action.
2. The course organizer (or another qualified individual) needs to ensure that the volunteer is robust enough, psychologically, to cope with discussing a personal problem in front of the training group.
3. Ongoing counselling should be made available, at reasonable cost, to the volunteer should he or she wish to continue therapy.
4. The volunteer should be told by the course organizer that the demonstration session will be discussed by the training course after it has finished, but that trainees will treat the material discussed in the interview in confidence — this means that they will not discuss the interview outside the training course.
5. If it is intended to record the interview, the purpose of the recording should be explained to the volunteer so that the volunteer can give

47

informed consent. If this is not forthcoming, the interview should not be recorded.

Having outlined these safeguards, let me present a transcript that I did with Linda on one of my training courses. I conducted the interview after I had outlined to trainees the basics of REBT theory and practice (see Chapter 1) and after I had discussed with them the REBT treatment sequence presented in the previous chapter.

While I will comment on this interview in the next chapter, you may wish to bear in mind the treatment sequence presented in the previous chapter as you read and study the interview as it was conducted.

The Interview

Windy: Thank you for coming today, Linda, and for agreeing to participate in this demonstration. What were you told about it?

Linda: I was told that volunteers were wanted to help you demonstrate the approach to counselling that you practise, that I would have to discuss a personal problem and that the students on your training course would be watching. I was also told that the transcript of our interview might be used later in a training book.

Windy: And is this acceptable to you?

Linda: Yes.

Windy: I want to add that if I do use your interview later in a book then I will change any identifying material and send the interview to you for your prior approval. Is that OK?

Linda: That's fine.

Windy: Also I believe that Peter [the course organizer] has arranged for some ongoing counselling for you should you want it later. Is that right?

Linda: Yes, that's right.

Windy: Good. Now what problem would you most like help with?

Linda: Well, there are two, I guess. There are a lot more [laughs], but two are particularly worrying me at the moment. First, my boyfriend. I'm having difficulties with him. We just seem to argue all the time these days and I'm pretty miserable about how things are going. Second, I'm having problems with my younger sister. She's very demanding at present and I find it difficult saying no to her.

Windy: Now, we may not have time to cover both today, so which one of these two problems do you want to focus on today, in particular?

Linda: Well, the situation with my boyfriend is worrying me the

	most, but it's quite complex so I guess . . . I guess I'll discuss my problems with my sister, Gillian.
Windy:	What's your problem with Gillian?
Linda:	Actually we call her Gill.
Windy:	Fine.
Linda:	Well, Gill has always been the black sheep of the family so to speak. She has always been in trouble. She got expelled at school. Actually she got expelled from two schools and she has had drug problems, drink problems and she has always screwed . . . I mean slept around.
Windy:	Actually, this shower in the audience can probably cope with the term 'screwed'. If they can't I'll kick them off the programme . . . [general laughter] . . . So use whatever language you're comfortable with. OK?
Linda:	OK. So, anyway, I think you get the picture about Gill.
Windy:	I think so. She probably won't win any daughter of the year contest . . .
Linda:	To say the least.
Windy:	To say the least.
Linda:	Well, recently, she has been making a real effort to get her stuff together. She's off drink and drugs and is going to one of those 12-step programmes and that seems to be helping her a lot.
Windy:	So she is doing well at the moment?
Linda:	She is, but the problem is that she is leaning on me heavily for support.
Windy:	Oh, I see.
Linda:	And, frankly, I think she's getting too dependent on me.
Windy:	Can you say briefly what support she seems to want from you?
Linda:	Well, she wants to use me like a counsellor. She expects me to listen to her problems endlessly and says that it is so useful to talk to me because otherwise she would get so wound up that she would do something stupid like taking drugs or going off to get drunk or something.
Windy:	And what's your problem about her doing this?
Linda:	Well, it's terribly draining to spend hours on the phone every night after a hard day's work. Also it's causing problems between Mike and me . . .
Windy:	I'm sorry, who's Mike?
Linda:	Oh, right, I never mentioned his name. Mike's my boyfriend.
Windy:	Oh, OK. So let me summarize, then. The problem as you see it is that Gill, your sister, is very dependent on you for support and wants to spend a lot of time telling you her problems. You find this very draining and it's beginning to lead to problems between you and your boyfriend, Mike. Is that accurate?

Linda: Very accurate.

Windy: Now, what would you like to achieve from our discussion with respect to the situation with Gill?

Linda: Well, I want her to stop leaning on me for support. I don't mind . . . No I want to be supportive to her, but I want her to ring me less.

Windy: So you want her to be less demanding. Now, it is important for me to be clear with you concerning what I can help you with and what I can't. Counselling can help you achieve what is in your control, but it can't really help you to achieve what is outside of your control. Does that make sense?

Linda: Yes, I think so.

Windy: Well, let me see if I can explain what I mean with respect to your problem with Gill. She phones you regularly and talks on the phone for a long time. Right?

Linda: Hm-hmm.

Windy: Now, when she decides to call you, who or what is causing her to do that?

Linda: She is.

Windy: And when she keeps talking who is responsible for that?

Linda: Well, we both are.

Windy: In what way?

Linda: Well, she is because she thinks she needs a lot of support, but I am because I don't say anything to her.

Windy: So if you said something to her what would that change?

Linda: Well, she wouldn't talk for so long.

Windy: Is that a probable outcome or something that will definitely happen?

Linda: A probable outcome.

Windy: So she could ignore what you say and keep on talking? That would be a possibility?

Linda: Yes, it would.

Windy: So is this a fair summary? Gill is responsible for ringing you in the first place and also for continuing to talk to you about her problems even though you may act to stop her. You are responsible for voicing your views on her dependent behaviour and what you want her to do about it. Voicing your views may or may not influence her behaviour. Is that accurate?

Linda: Yes it is.

Windy: Now, that is why I can't help her stop leaning on you for support nor can I help her ring you less often. These are behaviours that are within her control and not yours. Would you agree?

Linda: Yes.

Windy: Now, since Gill is not here and you are, does it make sense to focus on what you have control over?

Linda: Yes, it does.

Windy: Now, what do you think you can do that might help to reduce her dependency on you?

Linda: Well, I could be a lot firmer with Gill when she phones me. I could tell her how long I could talk to her for and I could tell her when next to ring.

Windy: Right, you could do these things and they may well help to reduce her dependency on you. They may be enough, but will you ever know if you don't put these limits to her?

Linda: No, I won't know.

Windy: And would you find it difficult to convey these limits to Gill?

Linda: I most certainly would.

Windy: Right, this often happens. People know what to do to help bring about a certain outcome, but they often stop themselves from taking that action. Now, let's suppose that you resolve to be clear with Gill about your limits the next time that she phones you; what emotion would you experience that would lead you not to say anything to her?

Linda: I'm not quite sure I understand what you mean.

Windy: Well, my hunch is that your resolve to tell Gill what your limits are would crumble during your next phone call and at that point you would experience an emotion that would be associated with the crumbling of your resolve to tell her about your limits.

Linda: Oh, I see. Right. I'd feel very anxious.

Windy: Anxious about what?

Linda: I'd be anxious that she'll get very upset about my limits and that in some way she might harm herself.

Windy: By doing what?

Linda: By going on a drinking binge, something like that.

Windy: And if she went on a drinking binge, how would you feel about that?

Linda: Very, very guilty.

Windy: Guilty about what?

Linda: For being responsible for her going on a binge.

Windy: So let me summarize. The reason that you don't tell Gill what your limits are is that you are scared that she might take what you say badly and go off on a binge of some sort and if she did that, you would feel very guilty because you would hold yourself responsible for her doing so.

Linda: That's exactly it.

Windy: Now, if we look at the problem this way, what do we need to tackle first?

Linda: I guess we need to help me to set limits in such a way that she doesn't go off on a binge.

Windy: Well, that would be an important point to address, but is Gill the type of person to react badly to you setting limits, no matter how wonderfully well you communicated them to her?

Linda: Yes, I get your point. Gill would think that I was rejecting her no matter how well I set out what my limits were.

Windy: Right, so we're left with your feelings of anxiety and guilt.

Linda: Well, I think that guilt is the real issue here. I often don't speak up for fear of hurting someone and when I do manage to get the courage up and tell someone how I feel, I feel terribly guilty if I hurt their feelings.

Windy: So, if I helped you over your guilt, then that would help you to set your limits with Gill?

Linda: [long pause] Well, I guess it would, but I don't want to be cold-hearted and uncaring.

Windy: I wouldn't want you to be that way either. However, the healthy alternative to guilt isn't being cold-hearted and uncaring. The healthy alternative to guilt is remorse, which means that you regret very much if Gill harms herself in response to you setting healthy limits, but you realize that you are looking after yourself while giving her an opportunity to get more healthy support for herself. Does that make sense?

Linda: So, I'd still feel bad if she were to go off on a binge?

Windy: Right, you'd feel bad, but that wouldn't stop you from setting healthy limits with Gill.

Linda: I've never thought about it in that way.

Windy: Right. So, would you like to commit yourself to feeling remorseful, but not guilty if Gill goes on a binge in response to your limit-setting?

Linda: Yes, that makes good sense.

Windy: OK. First, I want to clarify something. In this situation, would you feel more guilty about hurting Gill's feelings or about her going off on a binge?

Linda: In this situation, I would feel more guilty about her going off on a binge.

Windy: OK. Now, in the therapy that I practise, we use an ABC format for understanding people's problems. Now, let's apply this ABC format to your problem. OK?

Linda: OK.

Windy: I'll start with 'A' and 'C' first for reasons that will become clear in a moment. Now, 'A' stands for an activating event. This is the aspect of the situation you are most guilty about, which, in this instance, is causing your sister to go off on some kind of binge as a result of setting limits with her. Right?

Linda: Right.

Windy: 'C' stands for the emotions that you feel about 'A' and what you do in relation to 'A'. With me so far?

Linda: Yes, but why is it called 'C'?

Windy: 'C' really stands for Consequence — the emotional and behavioural consequences of something that I'll get to in a moment. OK?

Linda: Fine.

Windy: Now many people think that 'A' causes 'C', that it is the fact that you caused your sister to go off on a binge that in turn causes your guilt.

Linda: Are you saying that isn't the case?

Windy: I am. Let me show you what I mean. How would you feel if you believed: 'I don't care that I caused my sister to go off on a binge'?

Linda: I wouldn't feel anything.

Windy: And how would you feel if you believed: 'I'm glad that I caused my sister to go off on a binge'?

Linda: Then I'd guess I'd feel pleased, weird as it sounds.

Windy: So, is it the fact that you caused your sister to go off on a binge or is it your attitude of belief about doing that that is at the core of your feelings?

Linda: I see. Put like that, it's my attitude.

Windy: That's right. Paraphrasing Epictetus, an ancient philosopher: people are disturbed not by things, but because they have a certain set of beliefs or attitudes about those things. Now, let me see if I can help you to identify the beliefs that are at the core of your guilt. OK?

Linda: Fine.

Windy: Now, so far I've outlined two possible beliefs that you or any-one might have towards causing your sister to go off and have a binge and again let me stress that we are assuming for the moment that she does go on a binge of some sort after you have set limits with her and you are the direct cause of her behaviour. These beliefs are (1) indifference: 'I don't care if I caused her binge', and (2) a preference for something that is met: 'I want to cause her to binge and I am pleased that I have done so.' OK so far?

Linda: I'm with you.

Windy: Now, there are two other possible beliefs that you might have. I'll outline them and you tell me which best fits the belief that is at the core of your guilt. OK?

Linda: Fine.

Windy: The third possible belief that you may have is a preference that isn't met: 'I don't want to cause Gill to binge, but there is no reason why I must not do so. I'm very sorry that I did so.

That was wrong, but I'm not a bad person. Rather, I am a fallible human being who has done the wrong thing.'

The fourth and final belief that you may have is as follows: 'I absolutely must not cause Gill to binge and if I do this wrong thing I am a bad person for so doing.'

Now, do either of these two final beliefs fit the belief that is at the core of your guilt?

Linda: The final belief that you have just outlined sounds very much like what I do believe in relation to Gill.

Windy: Can you put it in your own words?

Linda: 'If Gill goes off on a drinking binge after I've told her what my limits are, then that is my fault. I really shouldn't have caused her to do this and I'm bad for doing so.'

Windy: Now with that belief is it any wonder why you don't attempt to set limits with her?

Linda: I guess not.

Windy: Now, let's assume once again that it is your fault that she went on a binge and that you caused this to happen. We'll have a closer look at these ideas later, but for the time being let's assume that that is so. Can you see that as long as you believe that you absolutely shouldn't have caused her to do so and that you are bad for doing so, that you will feel guilty after the fact and will avoid setting limits with her before the fact?

Linda: Yes, that's clear.

Windy: So, if you want to stop feeling guilty after the fact and if you want to set limits with Gill before the fact, what do you need to change?

Linda: The belief that I shouldn't have caused her to go on a binge and that I am bad for doing that.

Windy: Now, do you remember that you agreed to commit yourself to feeling remorseful rather than guilty should you have actually caused Gill's binge?

Linda: Yes, I do.

Windy: Now which of the other three beliefs that I have outlined do you think are at the core of remorse?

Linda: Can you run them by me again?

Windy: Sure. First there was the indifference belief. This can be expressed thus: 'I don't care whether or not I caused Gill's binge.' Now is that belief at the core of remorse?

Linda: No, not at all.

Windy: Right. Then there was the situation where your preference was met: 'I'm pleased that I caused Gill's binge.' Now, is that belief at the core of remorse?

Linda: No, I'd feel pleased if I believed that.

Windy: Right, so that just leaves us with the belief where your preference isn't met. If you recall, this belief can be expressed as follows: 'I really don't want to cause Gill's binge, but there is no reason why I absolutely shouldn't do so. I'm very sorry that I did so and that was wrong, but I'm not a bad person. I am a fallible human being who has done the wrong thing.' Now, do you think this belief is at the core of remorse?

Linda: Yes, if I believed that, then I would feel remorse . . .

Windy: But, not guilt.

Linda: No, not guilt.

Windy: So, what we need to do now is to help you to challenge the belief that is at the core of your guilt and help you to develop the belief that would be at the core of remorse. Does that make sense?

Linda: Perfect sense.

Windy: Now, I'll do this by asking you a number of questions designed to help you to question your guilt-related beliefs and in doing so we'll have a dialogue about these beliefs. OK?

Linda: OK.

Windy: Now let's take the belief that is at the core of your guilt, namely: 'I absolutely shouldn't have caused Gill to go on a binge and I am a bad person for doing that.' This belief is made up of two parts. The first part is 'I absolutely shouldn't have caused Gill to go on a binge', and the second part is 'I am a bad person for causing Gill to go on a binge.' Let's take them one at a time. OK?

Linda: Fine.

Windy: Now, where is the law of the universe that you absolutely must not cause Gill to go on a binge?

Linda: Well, it's the wrong thing to do.

Windy: Yes, it may well be the wrong thing to do, but why must you not do this wrong thing?

Linda: Because Gill will harm herself.

Windy: But that is a good answer to a different question. If I asked you why is it undesirable for you to do this wrong thing, what would you say?

Linda: I'd say the same thing: because Gill will harm herself.

Windy: Right, but I didn't ask you why it would be undesirable for you to cause Gill's binge. I asked you, in effect, whether or not there was a law of the universe which states that you absolutely must not cause her binge. Do you see?

Linda: Yes, I see what you're getting at. I can see that I have a must, but I can't quite get my head around your questions about this must.

Windy: Well, let me put it this way. Your preference not to cause Gill's binge indicates what you want and what you don't want and presumably you can prove why you don't want to cause her binge. Can't you?

Linda: Yes.

Windy: What are some of the reasons why you don't want to cause her to go on a binge?

Linda: Well, I love her. She's my sister and I want her to live a happy life.

Windy: Right, these are all good reasons in support of your belief: 'I don't want to cause Gill to binge.' But we know that you have another different belief. That is: 'I absolutely must not cause Gill to binge.' Now if such a law of the universe existed, how could you possibly cause her to binge?

Linda: Oh. Because the law would make it impossible to happen.

Windy: Right. You are, in fact, saying that the world must ensure that what you want is arranged. Is there any evidence that the world must ensure that you never cause Gill to binge?

Linda: No, of course not.

Windy: Right, so is your demand that you must not cause Gill to binge consistent or inconsistent with reality?

Linda: Inconsistent.

Windy: Because?

Linda: My demand is not an accurate reflection of how the world works.

Windy: Right, but your preference belief which can be stated thus: 'I really don't want to cause Gill to binge, but unfortunately there is no law which states that I must not do so.' Is that consistent or inconsistent with reality?

Linda: It's consistent with reality.

Windy: Because?

Linda: Because while it shows what I don't want to happen, it points to the fact that I may cause Gill to binge. It recognizes that there is no law preventing it from happening.

Windy: Good. That's what we call empirical disputing of your demand. We check whether or not your demand is consistent or inconsistent with reality. And we use the same check on your preference belief. Now, a second way of evaluating your demand is to see if it follows logically from your preference belief. So we know that you don't want to cause Gill to binge, but does it logically follow that therefore you must not do so?

Linda: Well, I guess not.

Windy: You don't sound too sure.

Linda: I guess I'm not.

Windy: Well, look at it this way. Do you play the lottery?

Linda: Yes.

Windy: Would you like to win the jackpot?

Linda: Of course I would.

Windy: Is it logical then for you to conclude that because you want to win the lottery therefore you have to do so?

Linda: Of course not

Windy: Why not?

Linda: Because what I want has no logical connection with what will happen.

Windy: Right. Your demand that you must not cause Gill to binge does not logically follow from your desire not to do so. But your desire is perfectly sensible, isn't it?

Linda: On its own, yes.

Windy: That is a really good point. On its own your desire is sensible; the illogicality comes in when you say: 'Because I don't want this to happen, therefore it must not.' Do you see that?

Linda: Yes, I do.

Windy: So that's what we call evaluating your demand along logical lines — and your desire, too. Now, the final way of evaluating your demand is along pragmatic lines. Now, what are the consequences for you when you demand that you absolutely must not cause Gill to go off on a binge?

Linda: I'd feel terribly guilty if I do actually cause her to binge . . .

Windy: Right . . .

Linda: And if I believe this then I won't be prepared even to attempt to set healthy limits with Gill, because I would be so scared that she would be upset even in response to my most gentle approach.

Windy: That's an excellent point, with the result that you will spend many hours helping her and, probably — we don't know for sure — but probably increasing her dependency on you. And would that be good for her or for you?

Linda: Most certainly not!

Windy: Right. Now, let's employ the same pragmatic argument to your desire. What will be the likely consequences for you if you believe: 'I really don't want to cause Gill to go out and binge, but unfortunately there is no law of the universe forbidding this from happening?'

Linda: Well, I would feel . . . what word did you call it? Oh, yes. I would feel remorse.

Windy: And would this belief stop you from setting healthy limits with Gill?

Linda: No, it wouldn't. I'd still feel concerned as I went about doing it, but, no, it wouldn't stop me.

Windy: That's right, it wouldn't stop you. In fact, it would encourage you to go carefully and probably reduce, but not eradicate, the risk that Gill will take what you say in a disturbed way.

	Can you see that?
Linda:	Yes, I can.
Windy:	So let's just recap on the work that we have just done. We've been helping you to re-evaluate the demand that is at the core of your avoidance and guilt. We've been using three criteria. Basically, is your demand that you must not cause Gill's binge consistent with reality? Is it logical? And does it bring about healthy results? And we concluded . . .?
Linda:	That my belief is not consistent with reality, that it is illogical and that it tends to bring about unhealthy results.
Windy:	And what did we conclude about your preference belief, namely: 'I would much prefer not to cause Gill's binge, but there is no law of the universe that states that I absolutely should not do so'?
Linda:	That it is consistent with reality, logical and leads to healthier results.
Windy:	At this point, you understand that your demand is self-defeating and your preference is healthier. Right?
Linda:	Right.
Windy:	Now, while this understanding is very important, on its own it won't necessarily help you set healthy limits with Gill and if you do manage to do this, this understanding won't on its own help you to feel remorse should you actually cause Gill to binge. Do you know why?
Linda:	While I can see these things, I don't truly believe them.
Windy:	Exactly. That's a very good insight. Now, while I can't help you to deepen your conviction in your preference belief and weaken your conviction in your demand in this one session, I will at the end give you some suggestions on how you can do this for yourself and, if you want to follow this up in ongoing therapy, as I said at the outset we can help set this up for you.
Linda:	Fine.
Windy:	But first I want us to consider the second part of your belief. Now, if I recall, your full belief was: 'I absolutely must not cause Gill to go off on a binge and if I do this wrong thing, then I am a bad person.' Is that right?
Linda:	Yes, that's right.
Windy:	So, let's take the second part of that belief, namely: 'I am a bad person if I do the wrong thing and cause Gill to go off and binge.' Now, remember we are still assuming that you can, in fact, cause Gill to go off and binge and that that is the wrong thing to do. Now, is it true that you are a bad person if you do this bad thing?
Linda:	Well, I wouldn't be a bad person if I didn't do it.
Windy:	But does doing this bad thing make you a bad person?

Linda: I guess not.

Windy: Why not?

Linda: I'm not sure.

Windy: Well, if you were a bad person through and through, what type of things could you only do?

Linda: Bad things?

Windy: That's right. Now, have you heard the phrase 'fallible human being'?

Linda: Yes.

Windy: What does it mean?

Linda: It means that you can make errors.

Windy: Right, it means that you can do bad things, good things and neutral things. Now, we have agreed that causing Gill to go off and binge is bad. But does that prove you are a bad person through and through or does it prove that you are a fallible human being who has done the wrong thing?

Linda: It proves that I'm fallible. But isn't that a cop-out?

Windy: What do you mean?

Linda: Well, doesn't saying: 'I'm a fallible human being' mean that I am excusing myself?

Windy: No, not at all. When you accept yourself as a fallible human being who has done the wrong thing, you are still acknowledging that you have done the wrong thing and you take full responsibility for your actions. In fact, accepting yourself in this way helps you to think carefully about reasons for your behaviour and to learn from the experience in future. Have you found that blaming or condemning yourself for your actions has helped you to think objectively about your behaviour and to learn from it?

Linda: No, putting it like that, I haven't found that at all. In fact, blaming myself has meant that I have been wrapped up entirely with my own guilt feelings.

Windy: And can you think objectively about the reasons for your behaviour when you are in the midst of guilt?

Linda: No. When I'm feeling guilty, I'm anything but objective. In fact, when I feel guilty I think only that things are my fault.

Windy: Precisely. So accepting yourself as a fallible human being achieves two things. It encourages you to take responsibility for your actions and helps you to think about your behaviour objectively and learn from it. So, can you see that telling yourself that you are a bad person is not only inconsistent with reality, but it will give you lousy results?

Linda: Yes, I can see that very clearly.

Windy: And can you also see that accepting yourself as a fallible human being while taking responsibility for your behaviour is true and more likely to give you sounder, healthier results?

Linda: Yes, you've persuaded me that that's the case.

Windy: So, one more question to go. Is it good logic to say that because you have done the wrong thing, therefore you are a bad person?

Linda: I'm not sure I know what you mean.

Windy: Well, we're assuming that you have caused Gill to go out and binge and that that is a bad thing to do. Right?

Linda: Right.

Windy: And would you agree that that one act is only a tiny fragment of your whole being?

Linda: Yes, I would.

Windy: Well, is it good logic to say that that small part of you makes the whole of you bad?

Linda: No, it certainly doesn't.

Windy: Right, that would be making the part–whole error, where you define the whole of something on the basis of a part of it. But is it logical to conclude that you are fallible human being — a mixture of good, bad and neutral aspects — for acting badly by making Gill go out and binge?

Linda: Yes, that is logical.

Windy: So, let's recap on the work that we have done on the second part of your belief, which was that you would be a bad person if you caused Gill to go out and binge. Again, we looked at that belief in terms of whether it is consistent with reality, logical and functional. And what did we conclude?

Linda: That it was none of those things, but that the alternative belief where I accept myself as a fallible human for having done the wrong thing is true, logical and . . . what was the last thing?

Windy: Functional . . .

Linda: Functional . . . that it will give me better results.

Windy: Now, remember what I said earlier. Just knowing all this isn't enough. You need to really believe it. Now, let me give you two suggestions concerning how you can weaken your conviction in your unhealthy belief and deepen your conviction in the healthy alternative. OK?

Linda: I'm all ears.

Windy: Now, the first thing that you can do is take the healthy belief: 'I really would prefer not to have caused Gill to go on a binge, but unfortunately there is no law of the universe to say that I must not do so. If I do so, then I can still accept myself as a fallible human being who has done a very wrong thing.' Then write it down on a piece of paper. Second, rate how much you really believe it on a scale of 0–100%. Third, write down something that attacks that belief using any argument that occurs to you. Fourth, respond to this attack with a plausible argument, ripping it up. Proceed in this way until you have responded to all the attacks you can think of and then re-rate your conviction in the original healthy belief you started with. If you do the exercise properly you should increase your conviction in the new, healthy belief. Is that clear?

Linda: Yes, but it is a lot to take in in one go.

Windy: Right, so I'll give you a written list of these instructions at the end of the session.

Linda: Oh, good.

Windy: Now, a second way of increasing your conviction in the healthy belief is to act on it. You may not want to do so immediately with Gill. But can you think of a less challenging example where you can assert yourself and practise the new belief before, during and after doing so?

Linda: . . . Yes, I can think of something.

Windy: Tell me.

Linda: Well, I have a friend that I find it hard to say no to. So, the next time she asks me for a favour, I can refuse to do it.

Windy: Now, the important thing about doing this, which we call a behavioural exercise, is that you practise your new belief while doing so. So what will you tell yourself before you turn her down?

Linda: Well, I can remind myself that I have a right to say no . . .

Windy: . . . And if you, so to speak, hurt her feelings?

Linda: Well, I wouldn't like it, but I can accept myself for doing so. There's no law to prevent me from hurting her feelings. But I'm not doing so maliciously.

Windy: Right. And you can rehearse this belief after the fact, too, whether or not you, in quotes, 'hurt her feelings'. Now, do you think that doing this would be good preparation for what you need to say to your sister?

Linda: Yes, that would help a lot.

Windy: So will you agree to assert yourself with your friend?

Linda: Yes, I will.

Windy: Now, there is one more issue that I want to raise with you before we finish. OK?

Linda: Hm-hmm.

Windy: Throughout this interview we have accepted your point that you can, in fact, cause Gill to go off and binge. Now, the reason I have taken this tack is because it has let us identify the beliefs that are at the core of your guilt and which help prevent you from asserting yourself with Gill. In my book, *Overcoming Guilt* (Dryden, 1994), I suggest that whenever you feel guilty about doing something, for example, you assume temporarily that you did, in fact, do it, that it was bad and thst you are responsible for doing it. Then you identify and challenge the ideas that are at the core of your guilt. Once you have done this then you are likely to be in a better frame of mind to consider objectively whether or not you can be said to cause Gill to go off and binge if she does so after you have set limits with her. You can't easily do this when you are feeling guilty. Am I making myself clear?

Linda: I think so.

Windy: Can you put that into your own words?

Linda: You're saying that when you feel guilt it is important to assume for the moment that you have done something wrong. And you wait until you have found and questioned your beliefs before looking at whether or not you are to blame.

Windy: Excellent, although I would say whether you are responsible, rather than to blame.

Linda: I see.

Windy: Now, let's suppose that you do lay down clear boundaries with Gill and let's suppose that she does go off and binge. Who is responsible for what?

Linda: Well, I guess it depends on how I say it to her.

Windy: That's a good point. If you set limits in a hostile way, you do increase the chances that Gill will go on a binge, but even here can you be said to cause her behaviour?

Linda: I guess not.

Windy: Why not?

Linda: Because, theoretically anyway, it is her beliefs about what I said that would lead her to binge.

Windy: Why theoretically?

Linda: Because I know Gill and if I was hostile to her, she would definitely go out and binge. She'll probably do so even if I am nice.

Windy: But does that mean that you cause her behaviour or that she very easily causes her own behaviour?

Linda: That she easily causes her own behaviour.

Windy: Now, because she is so vulnerable, you will need to take extra care in what you say to her. Right?

Linda: Right.

Windy: But, if you do take care and she goes off on a binge, who is primarily responsible for this?

Linda: She is.

Windy: Right, you are responsible for what you know about Gill and for how you address the issue of limit-setting with her. But she is responsible for her beliefs, her feelings and her behaviour. The fact that she is basically responsible for going on a binge doesn't give you *carte blanche* over how you treat her. But it does mean that if you set limits in a sensitive way and she responds by going on a binge, she is basically responsible for doing so. Can you see that?

Linda: Yes. But I'll still feel badly if she does so.

Windy: Right, it's healthy to feel concerned about such a possibility. Now, before we close let me stress that in order to get over your guilt and avoidance, assume temporarily that you did cause Gill's binge and after you've done that remind yourself about who is responsible for what in the event of her binge. OK?

Linda: OK.

Windy: Good luck with saying no to your friend.

Linda: Thanks.

Windy: And thank you for coming here today.

Linda: Thank you for your help.

Chapter 4
Commentary on Windy Dryden's Demonstration Session

In this chapter, I will provide an ongoing commentary on the demonstration session that was presented in the previous chapter. In doing so I will use the REBT treatment sequence discussed in Chapter 2 as the framework for my comments.

Interview with Commentary

Windy: Thank you for coming today, Linda, and for agreeing to participate in this demonstration. What were you told about it?

Linda: I was told that volunteers were wanted to help you demonstrate the approach to counselling that you practise, that I would have to discuss a personal problem and that the students on your training course would be watching. I was also told that the transcript of our interview might be used later in a training book.

Windy: And is this acceptable to you?

Linda: Yes.

Windy: I want to add that if I do use your interview later in a book then I will change any identifying material and send the interview to you for your prior approval. Is that OK?

Linda: That's fine.

Windy: Also I believe that Peter [the course organizer] has arranged for some ongoing counselling for you should you want it later. Is that right?

Linda: Yes, that's right.

[As discussed on pp. 47–48, when someone from outside the training course is invited to assume the role of client and discuss a personal problem in front of the training group, certain safeguards need to be in place. I ascertain from Linda that she understands that the session is a demonstration of REBT, that it will be in front of the training group and that the transcript of the interview may be used later in a book. I then stress that if I want to use the interview for publication I will change any identifying material and seek her permission to publish the interview. I did, in fact, send Linda the transcript and asked her to make any changes she wanted. She made only a couple of minor changes and gave her written permission for the interview to be used in the form in which it appears in this book and for it to be subject to analysis.

I also stressed that she would be offered ongoing counselling should she request it. In fact, she was seen for five sessions by a local, trained REBT therapist.

I failed to make the point at the beginning of the session that the session would be treated in confidence by the training group. Although the course organizer did make this clear to Linda when she was invited to volunteer, I wish that I had stressed this point at the outset.]

Windy: Good. Now what problem would you most like help with?

[Having established the ground rules for the interview, I immediately become problem-focused and ask Linda for the problem that she would most like help with (Sequence: Step 1).]

Linda: Well, there are two, I guess. There are a lot more [laughs], but two are particularly worrying me at the moment. First, my boyfriend. I'm having difficulties with him. We just seem to argue all the time these days and I'm pretty miserable about how things are going. Second, I'm having problems with my younger sister. She's very demanding at present and I find it difficult saying no to her.

[Note that Linda responds by identifying two problems that she would like help with. Knowing that I will probably not have time to discuss both with her in a single session, I ask her to choose one of these problems for particular attention.]

Windy: Now, we may not have time to cover both today, so which one of these two problems do you want to focus on today, in particular?
Linda: Well, the situation with my boyfriend is worrying me the most, but it's quite complex so I guess . . . I guess I'll discuss my problems with my sister, Gillian.
Windy: What's your problem with Gillian?
Linda: Actually we call her Gill.
Windy: Fine.

Linda: Well, Gill has always been the black sheep of the family so to
           speak. She has always been in trouble. She got expelled at
           school. Actually she got expelled from two schools and she
           has had drug problems, drink problems and she has always
           screwed . . . I mean slept around.
Windy: Actually, this shower in the audience can probably cope with
           the term 'screwed'. If they can't I'll kick them off the pro-
           gramme . . . [general laughter] . . . So use whatever language
           you're comfortable with. OK?

[I deliberately make this somewhat provocative, humorous remark to put
Linda at her ease. I do not want her to monitor her language and this
intervention helps to diffuse her tension and 'gives permission' to Linda
that it is perfectly OK to use vulgarisms. By now, the training group
would have grown accustomed to my use of humour and by their general
laughter they show that they appreciate what I am trying to achieve.]

Linda: OK. So, anyway, I think you get the picture about Gill.
Windy: I think so. She probably won't win any daughter of the year
           contest . . .
Linda: To say the least.
Windy: To say the least.
Linda: Well, recently, she has been making a real effort to get her
           stuff together. She's off drink and drugs and is going to one of
           those 12-step programmes and that seems to be helping her a
           lot.
Windy: So she is doing well at the moment?
Linda: She is, but the problem is that she is leaning on me heavily for
           support.

[Up to this point, I am quite content for Linda to express herself in her
own way. In single demonstrations of REBT, the role of the therapist is
to strike the right balance between giving the client an opportunity to
discuss her concerns in her own way on the one hand, and using the
structure of REBT on the other. This tension is more acute in one-off
demonstrations where time is limited than in ongoing REBT. However,
it is also an issue in ongoing therapy and it is important that you bear
this in mind in your continuing work with clients.]

Windy: Oh, I see.
Linda: And, frankly, I think she's getting too dependent on me.
Windy: Can you say briefly what support she seems to want from you?
Linda: Well, she wants to use me like a counsellor. She expects me to
           listen to her problems endlessly and says that it is so useful to
           talk to me because otherwise she would get so wound up that

	she would do something stupid like taking drugs or going off to get drunk or something.
Windy:	And what's your problem about her doing this?
Linda:	Well, it's terribly draining to spend hours on the phone every night after a hard day's work. Also it's causing problems between Mike and me . . .
Windy:	I'm sorry, who's Mike?
Linda:	Oh, right, I never mentioned his name. Mike's my boyfriend.
Windy:	Oh, OK. So let me summarize, then. The problem as you see it is that Gill, your sister, is very dependent on you for support and wants to spend a lot of time telling you her problems. You find this very draining and it's beginning to lead to problems between you and your boyfriend, Mike. Is that accurate?
Linda:	Very accurate.

[As discussed on pp. 20–23, it is very important that you and your client agree on the client's problem as defined by the client. Otherwise, misunderstandings may well occur and lead to problems in the therapeutic alliance between you and your client. Note that I use a summarizing statement to check out my understanding of Linda's defined problem and further note that in the following response, she confirms that my summary is accurate (Sequence: Step 2).]

Windy:	Now, what would you like to achieve from our discussion with respect to the situation with Gill?

[At this point I ask Linda about her goals for change in line with her problem as defined.]

Linda:	Well, I want her to stop leaning on me for support. I don't mind . . . No I want to be supportive to her, but I want her to ring me less.
Windy:	So you want her to be less demanding. Now, it is important for me to be clear with you concerning what I can help you with and what I can't. Counselling can help you achieve what is in your control, but it can't really help you to achieve what is outside of your control. Does that make sense?

[On pp. 29–31, I discussed the characteristics of client goals that REBT therapists agree to work towards with their clients. I stressed that it is important that the client's goals are within her control. Note that in response to my question about her goal, Linda states that she wants her sister to ring her less and stop leaning on her for support. As these are outside Linda's direct control, I decide to spend some time on this issue. The point that I want to make is that Linda may be able to influence Gill to be less demanding on her and as these influence attempts are within Linda's direct control, they are acceptable as goals in REBT. However, the result of these attempts, Gill's responses, are not within Linda's direct control and are therefore not acceptable as goals in REBT. The following dialogue represents my rather cumbersome attempt at clarifying these issues with Linda.]

Linda: Yes, I think so.

Windy: Well, let me see if I can explain what I mean with respect to your problem with Gill. She phones you regularly and talks on the phone for a long time. Right?

Linda: Hm-hmm.

Windy: Now, when she decides to call you, who or what is causing her to do that?

Linda: She is.

Windy: And when she keeps talking who is responsible for that?

Linda: Well, we both are.

Windy: In what way?

Linda: Well, she is because she thinks she needs a lot of support, but I am because I don't say anything to her.

Windy: So if you said something to her what would that change?

Linda: Well, she wouldn't talk for so long.

Windy: Is that a probable outcome or something that will definitely happen?

Linda: A probable outcome.

Windy: So she could ignore what you say and keep on talking? That would be a possibility?

Linda: Yes, it would.

Windy: So is this a fair summary? Gill is responsible for ringing you in the first place and also for continuing to talk to you about her problems even though you may act to stop her. You are responsible for voicing your views on her dependent behaviour and what you want her to do about it. Voicing your views may or may not influence her behaviour. Is that accurate?

Linda: Yes it is.

Windy: Now, that is why I can't help her stop leaning on you for support nor can I help her ring you less often. These are behaviours that are within her control and not yours. Would you agree?

Linda: Yes.

Windy: Now, since Gill is not here and you are, does it make sense to focus on what you have control over?

Linda: Yes, it does.

Windy: Now, what do you think you can do that might help to reduce her dependency on you?

[Having discussed the issue of goals that are within Linda's direct control and those that are not and having ascertained that she understands this distinction, I proceed to ask her to specify what she could do that may result in Gill's decreased dependency on her.]

Linda: Well, I could be a lot firmer with Gill when she phones me. I could tell her how long I could talk to her for and I could tell her when next to ring.

Windy: Right, you could do these things and they may well help to reduce her dependency on you. They may be enough, but will you ever know if you don't put these limits to her?

Linda: No, I won't know.

Windy: And would you find it difficult to convey these limits to Gill?

Linda: I most certainly would.

Windy: Right, this often happens. People know what to do to help bring about a certain outcome, but they often stop themselves from taking that action. Now, let's suppose that you resolve to be clear with Gill about your limits the next time that she phones you; what emotion would you experience that would lead you not to say anything to her?

[My hypothesis at this stage of the interview was that while Gill may be aware of what to do to set limits with her sister, her real problem is that she stops herself from doing so for psychological reasons. So what I am doing here is this. I am attempting to assess Linda's C (Sequence: Step 3), which here is the emotion that she would begin to experience when she moves towards limit-setting with Gill that would lead her to back away from doing so. This is quite a complicated idea and, as Linda's following response shows, I fail to make myself clear the first time I raise the issue.]

Linda: I'm not quite sure I understand what you mean.

Windy: Well, my hunch is that your resolve to tell Gill what your limits are would crumble during your next phone call and at that point you would experience an emotion that would be associated with the crumbling of your resolve to tell her about your limits.

[As Linda's following response shows, this second attempt to get at her C is successful.]

Linda: Oh, I see. Right. I'd feel very anxious.

Windy: Anxious about what?

[Having identified Linda's C — anxiety — I now begin to ask questions to identify her critical A (see pp. 26–29). As you will recall, the critical A is the A in the total complex that triggers the client's irrational beliefs that are at the core of her target C. In my mind I am also conceptualizing Linda's crumbling resolve and her subsequent failure to set limits with Gill as a behavioural C associated with her anxiety.]

Linda: I'd be anxious that she'll get very upset about my limits and that in some way she might harm herself.
Windy: By doing what?
Linda: By going on a drinking binge, something like that.
Windy: And if she went on a drinking binge, how would you feel about that?

[You may be wondering why I ask for Linda's C at this point rather than continuing the inference chain related to anxiety, for example by asking. 'And what would be anxiety-provoking in your mind about Gill going on a drinking binge?' I could certainly have done this but let me explain my reasons for taking the route that I did.

When a person is anxious, she is anxious either about a future threat or about the future threatening implications of a present event. Now note that in the response above I have brought a future threat into the past: 'And if she WENT on a drinking binge . . .' I am also aware of my hypothesis about the real nature of Linda's problem; namely she stops herself from asserting herself with Gill because she would feel guilty about the possible outcome of such assertion. As DiGiuseppe (1991) notes, REBT therapists' assessment interventions are guided by the hypotheses that they form about their clients' utterances. Thus, my hypothesis led me to ask about Linda's new C at this point rather than to continue the anxiety-related inference chain. Thus, although I had indicated a search for Linda's critical A related to anxiety, I return to Step 3 of the sequence because the A I identified is now in the past.]

Linda: Very, very guilty.
Windy: Guilty about what?

[Once I have ascertained Linda's new C, I immediately enquire about her new A (Sequence: Indicating Step 4).]

Linda: For being responsible for her going on a binge.

[Rather than initiate a new 'guilt-driven' inference chain, I decide at this point to summarize the work we have done up to this point. I do this because I still need to ascertain from Linda which emotion – anxiety or guilt – she regards as more central to her problem.]

Windy: So let me summarize. The reason that you don't tell Gill what your limits are is that you are scared that she might take what

you say badly and go off on a binge of some sort and if she
did that, you would feel very guilty because you would hold
yourself responsible for her doing so.

Linda: That's exactly it.

Windy: Now, if we look at the problem this way, what do we need to
tackle first?

[My question is too vague. A better question would have been: 'Do we
need to tackle your anxiety first or your guilt?']

Linda: I guess we need to help me to set limits in such a way that she
doesn't go off on a binge.

[Although my question is vague it does reveal that Linda is still looking
for a way to behave that would get rid of her feared A (Gill's binge).
This gives me another opportunity to address the unrealistic nature of
this goal.]

Windy: Well, that would be an important point to address, but is Gill
the type of person to react badly to you setting limits, no matter how wonderfully well you communicated them to her?

Linda: Yes, I get your point. Gill would think that I was rejecting her
no matter how well I set out what my limits were.

Windy: Right, so we're left with your feelings of anxiety and guilt.

[Linda's response enables me to return to the target C (Sequence: Step 3).]

Linda: Well, I think that guilt is the real issue here. I often don't
speak up for fear of hurting someone and when I do manage
to get the courage up and tell someone how I feel, I feel terribly guilty if I hurt their feelings.

[Linda reveals that guilt is her target unhealthy negative emotion.]

Windy: So, if I helped you over your guilt, then that would help you
to set your limits with Gill?

[I ask this question to check that she would be able to assert herself
with her sister if she did not experience the target C.

Linda: [long pause] Well, I guess it would, but I don't want to be
cold-hearted and uncaring.

[In her answer, Linda reveals that she does not see clearly what a
healthy response to her sister going off on a binge would be. She thinks

that the only alternative to feeling guilt is to be 'cold-hearted'. Unless I correct her misconception, it is unlikely that she will be motivated to change her guilt.]

Windy: I wouldn't want you to be that way either. However, the healthy alternative to guilt isn't being cold-hearted and uncaring. The healthy alternative to guilt is remorse, which means that you regret very much if Gill harms herself in response to you setting healthy limits, but you realize that you are looking after yourself while giving her an opportunity to get more healthy support for herself. Does that make sense?
Linda: So, I'd still feel bad if she were to go off on a binge?
Windy: Right, you'd feel bad, but that wouldn't stop you from setting healthy limits with Gill.
Linda: I've never thought about it in that way.

[This response shows that Linda has understood my point about remorse being a healthy alternative to guilt.]

Windy: Right. So, would you like to commit yourself to feeling remorseful, but not guilty if Gill goes on a binge in response to your limit-setting?

[I immediately ask Linda if she wishes to commit herself to her new emotional goal of being remorseful if Gill responds to her assertion by binging. This represents goal-setting in line with the problem as assessed (see pp. 29–30). Although you will note that I have not fully assessed Linda's problem at this point, I have her target C, which is the minimum information that I need to do this.]

Linda: Yes, that makes good sense.
Windy: OK. First, I want to clarify something. In this situation, would you feel more guilty about hurting Gill's feelings or about her going off on a binge?

[Instead of doing a full inference chain with guilt as the driving emotion, I use my knowledge of guilt (Dryden, 1994) to guide my question at this point. I know that Linda would hold herself responsible for Gill's response to her limit setting for she has told me so above. I need to know at this point whether her critical A is 'Hurting Gill's feelings' or 'Causing her to go off on a binge'. To ascertain this I ask her direct.]

Linda: In this situation, I would feel more guilty about her going off on a binge.

[This then represents her critical A (Sequence: Completing Step 4).]

Windy: OK. Now, in the therapy that I practise, we use an ABC format for understanding people's problems. Now, let's apply this ABC format to your problem. OK?

[Although I have assessed Linda's A and C, I still have to teach her about the ABCs of REBT and how this accounts for her problem. So I decide that now is a good time to adopt a more educational stance. Note that I ask permission before I do this.]

Linda: OK.
Windy: I'll start with 'A' and 'C' first for reasons that will become clear in a moment. Now, 'A' stands for an activating event. This is the aspect of the situation you are most guilty about, which, in this instance, is causing your sister to go off on some kind of binge as a result of setting limits with her. Right?
Linda: Right.
Windy: 'C' stands for the emotions that you feel about 'A' and what you do in relation to 'A'. With me so far?
Linda: Yes, but why is it called 'C'?
Windy: 'C' really stands for Consequence — the emotional and behavioural consequences of something that I'll get to in a moment. OK?
Linda: Fine.
Windy: Now many people think that 'A' causes 'C', that it is the fact that you caused your sister to go off on a binge that in turn causes your guilt.

[Having reviewed the work that I have already done with Linda and introduced the meaning of A and C, I am now ready to teach Linda the specific principle of emotional responsibility where irrational beliefs are seen to be at the core of people's emotional problems (see Dryden, 1995a, for a full discussion of this issue). There are many ways of teaching clients this principle (also known as the iB-C connection — Sequence: Step 6) and I list a number of such methods in another book in this series (Dryden, 1995a). As you will see, I choose to teach Linda this principle by showing her that there are four different beliefs that it is possible to hold about her A: (1) indifference; (2) a met preference (where a desired A occurs); (3) an unmet preference (where a desired A does not occur); and (4) a demand. This method is closest to the four surgeon technique described in Dryden (1995a), but uses the client's own example as teaching material.]

Linda: Are you saying that isn't the case?

Windy: I am. Let me show you what I mean. How would you feel if
          you believed: 'I don't care that I caused my sister to go off on
          a binge'?

[This is indifference.]

Linda: I wouldn't feel anything.
Windy: And how would you feel if you believed: 'I'm glad that I
          caused my sister to go off on a binge'?

[This is the met preference.]

Linda: Then I'd guess I'd feel pleased, weird as it sounds.
Windy: So, is it the fact that you caused your sister to go off on a
          binge or is it your attitude of belief about doing that that is at
          the core of your feelings?
Linda: I see. Put like that, it's my attitude.

[I decide to make my major point after presenting Linda with two of the
four belief possibilities. If she had not understood it, I would have
introduced the other two possibilities at this point. As she does understand my point, I decide to reinforce it by referring to Epictetus' famous
dictum.]

Windy: That's right. Paraphrasing Epictetus, an ancient philosopher:
          people are disturbed not by things, but because they have a
          certain set of beliefs or attitudes about those things. Now, let
          me see if I can help you to identify the beliefs that are at the
          core of your guilt. OK?
Linda: Fine.

[Linda is now ready to understand the belief that is at the core of her
guilt. Because I also want her to understand the belief that is at the core
of remorse (her emotional goal), I introduce these two beliefs in one
chunk. This enables me to stress the differences between an unmet
preference and a demand.]

Windy: Now, so far I've outlined two possible beliefs that you or any-
          one might have towards causing your sister to go off and have
          a binge and again let me stress that we are assuming for the
          moment that she does go on a binge of some sort after you
          have set limits with her and you are the direct cause of her
          behaviour. These beliefs are (1) indifference: 'I don't care if I
          caused her binge', and (2) a preference for something that is
          met: 'I want to cause her to binge and I am pleased that I
          have done so.' OK so far?

[Note that I introduce a radical idea here that I will reiterate several times throughout the remainder of the session. I tell Linda that we will assume temporarily that she did cause her sister's binge. This is known in REBT as assuming that A is true (see p. 28). Making this assumption enables us to work towards identifying Linda's irrational belief that is at the core of her guilt. In working with clients at this point, you may well be tempted to dispute her inference (in Linda's case that she caused her sister's binge). It is important that you resist this temptation so that you can identify your clients' irrational beliefs.]

Linda: I'm with you.
Windy: Now, there are two other possible beliefs that you might have. I'll outline them and you tell me which best fits the belief that is at the core of your guilt. OK?
Linda: Fine.
Windy: The third possible belief that you may have is a preference that isn't met: 'I don't want to cause Gill to binge, but there is no reason why I must not do so. I'm very sorry that I did so. That was wrong, but I'm not a bad person. Rather, I am a fallible human being who has done the wrong thing.'
          The fourth and final belief that you may have is as follows: 'I absolutely must not cause Gill to binge and if I do this wrong thing I am a bad person for so doing.'
          Now, do either of these two final beliefs fit the belief that is at the core of your guilt?

[Although I have chosen a didactic mode of helping Linda to identify her irrational belief (Sequence: Step 7), I am encouraging her to be active in the process by asking her forced-choice questions. Let me stress one other point here. You will notice that I imply that her irrational belief is AT THE CORE of her guilt. I do not say that this belief CAUSES her guilt. Ellis (1962) has stressed at the outset that beliefs, feelings and behaviour are interdependent processes and that beliefs are central to an understanding of our emotions. The phrase 'at the core of' does full justice to these two central ideas of REBT.]

Linda: The final belief that you have just outlined sounds very much like what I do believe in relation to Gill.
Windy: Can you put it in your own words?

[Again note that I am urging Linda to be as active as possible within the didactic teaching paradigm.]

Linda: 'If Gill goes off on a drinking binge after I've told her what my limits are, then that is my fault. I really shouldn't have caused

	her to do this and I'm bad for doing so.'
Windy:	Now, with that belief is it any wonder why you don't attempt to set limits with her?

[Here I am emphasizing the iB-C connection — that her irrational belief inhibits assertion (Sequence: Step 8).]

Linda:	I guess not.
Windy:	Now let's assume once again that it is your fault that she went on a binge and that you caused this to happen. We'll have a closer look at these ideas later, but for the time being let's assume that that is so. Can you see that as long as you believe that you absolutely shouldn't have caused her to do so and that you are bad for doing so, that you will feel guilty after the fact and will avoid setting limits with her before the fact?

[I reiterate the iB-C connection, this time showing Linda that holding her irrational belief is associated with guilt as well as inhibiting assertion.]

Linda:	Yes, that's clear.
Windy:	So, if you want to stop feeling guilty after the fact and if you want to set limits with Gill before the fact, what do you need to change?

[This question is designed to help Linda to see that we need to help her to change her irrational belief if she is to achieve her goal.]

Linda:	The belief that I shouldn't have caused her to go on a binge and that I am bad for doing that.
Windy:	Now, do you remember that you agreed to commit yourself to feeling remorseful rather than guilty should you have actually caused Gill's binge?
Linda:	Yes, I do.
Windy:	Now which of the other three beliefs that I have outlined do you think are at the core of remorse?

[Here I am endeavouring to help Linda connect her goals with her rational belief (what might be called the rB-C connection).]

Linda:	Can you run them by me again?
Windy:	Sure. First there was the indifference belief. This can be expressed thus: 'I don't care whether or not I caused Gill's binge.' Now is that belief at the core of remorse?
Linda:	No, not at all.

Windy: Right. Then there was the situation where your preference
          was met: 'I'm pleased that I caused Gill's binge.' Now, is that
          belief at the core of remorse?
Linda: No, I'd feel pleased if I believed that.
Windy: Right, so that just leaves us with the belief where your prefer-
          ence isn't met. If you recall, this belief can be expressed as fol-
          lows: 'I really don't want to cause Gill's binge, but there is no
          reason why I absolutely shouldn't do so. I'm very sorry that I
          did so and that was wrong, but I'm not a bad person. I am a
          fallible human being who has done the wrong thing.' Now, do
          you think this belief is at the core of remorse?
Linda: Yes, if I believed that, then I would feel remorse . . .
Windy: But, not guilt.

[Note that I check to see that Linda clearly differentiates the consequences of her rational belief from those that stem from her irrational
belief.]

Linda: No, not guilt.
Windy: So, what we need to do now is to help you to challenge the
          belief that is at the core of your guilt and help you to develop
          the belief that would be at the core of remorse. Does that
          make sense?

[Here I prepare the ground to dispute Linda's irrational belief and to
help her to acquire the rational alternative. I am also reiterating the rB-
C connection.]

Linda: Perfect sense.
Windy: Now, I'll do this by asking you a number of questions designed
          to help you to question your guilt-related beliefs and in doing
          so we'll have a dialogue about these beliefs. OK?

[Note that I explain what I will be doing in the disputing stage (Sequence:
Step 9).]

Linda: OK.
Windy: Now let's take the belief that is at the core of your guilt,
          namely: 'I absolutely shouldn't have caused Gill to go on a
          binge and I am a bad person for doing that.' This belief is
          made up of two parts. The first part is 'I absolutely shouldn't
          have caused Gill to go on a binge', and the second part is 'I
          am a bad person for causing Gill to go on a binge.' Let's take
          them one at a time. OK?

[A full irrational belief has two parts, a demand and one or more derivatives from the demand (awfulizing, low frustration tolerance and self-
downing) — see Dryden (1995a) for a fuller discussion of this point.
What I shall be doing in the disputing phase of the interview is to deal
with each part separately. I begin by disputing Linda's demanding belief
because according to REBT theory this belief is at the very core of her
guilt. Note that I predominantly adopt a Socratic style of questioning in
the following sequence (see Dryden, 1995b, for a discussion of Socratic
and didactic disputing.]

Linda: Fine.
Windy: Now, where is the law of the universe that you absolutely
           must not cause Gill to go on a binge?

[There are three major arguments that you can employ when disputing
your client's irrational beliefs: empirical, logical and pragmatic arguments (DiGiuseppe, 1991). In the following exchanges you will note
that I keep these arguments separate. I do so for two reasons. First, I
believe that this helps the client to think things through for herself. Second, it helps trainee REBT therapists to gain a clear understanding of
the disputing process. If I mixed up the three arguments, then both
client and trainee are likely to become confused.]

Linda: Well, it's the wrong thing to do.

[Here Linda does not address herself to my question. Indeed, she is
probably answering a different question, one that I did not ask; namely:
Why is it undesirable for you to cause Gill to go on a binge? I have a
choice of two responses. I could say: 'That's evidence for it being undesirable to cause her to binge' and then repeat my original question. Or I
could do what I, in fact, did; namely, challenge the demand as it now
relates to the more abstract concept of 'doing this wrong thing. It may
have been better to have done the former, but there is no compelling
reason to favour one response over the other at this point (see
DiGiuseppe, 1991, for a discussion of disputing specific and abstract
irrational beliefs).]

Windy: Yes, it may well be the wrong thing to do, but why must you
           not do this wrong thing?
Linda: Because Gill will harm herself.
Windy: But that is a good answer to a different question. If I asked
           you why is it undesirable for you to do this wrong thing, what
           would you say?

[Note that here I use the first strategy discussed above.]

Linda: I'd say the same thing: because Gill will harm herself.
Windy: Right, but I didn't ask you why it would be undesirable for you to cause Gill's binge. I asked you, in effect, whether or not there was a law of the universe that states that you absolutely must not cause her binge. Do you see?
Linda: Yes, I see what you're getting at. I can see that I have a must, but I can't quite get my head around your questions about this must.

[Do not be alarmed if your client becomes confused during the disputing process. You are introducing new concepts to her, which she may have difficulty grasping at first. In which case, keep calm and try and find an alternative, clearer way of explaining your point. In addition, as you are encouraging her to think for herself, it is important to go slowly.]

Windy: Well, let me put it this way. Your preference not to cause Gill's binge indicates what you want and what you don't want and presumably you can prove why you don't want to cause her binge. Can't you?
Linda: Yes.
Windy: What are some of the reasons why you don't want to cause her to go on a binge?
Linda: Well, I love her. She's my sister and I want her to live a happy life.
Windy: Right, these are all good reasons in support of your belief: 'I don't want to cause Gill to binge.' But we know that you have another different belief. That is: 'I absolutely must not cause Gill to binge.' Now if such a law of the universe existed, how could you possibly cause her to binge?

[By asking Linda to list the reasons why she does not want to cause her sister's binge, I am showing her that these are all good empirical reasons in support of her preference. I follow this up by asking her what would happen empirically if her demand existed.]

Linda: Oh. Because the law would make it impossible to happen.

[Linda seems to understand the point, so I reinforce it below.]

Windy: Right. You are, in fact, saying that the world must ensure that what you want is arranged. Is there any evidence that the world must ensure that you never cause Gill to binge?

Linda: No, of course not.
Windy: Right, so is your demand that you must not cause Gill to binge consistent or inconsistent with reality?
Linda: Inconsistent.
Windy: Because?
Linda: My demand is not an accurate reflection of how the world works.

[Linda now clearly seems to understand the point that there is no empirical evidence in support of a demand.]

Windy: Right, but your preference belief which can be stated thus: 'I really don't want to cause Gill to binge, but unfortunately there is no law which states that I must not do so.' Is that consistent or inconsistent with reality?

[Having employed the empirical criterion to Linda's must, I now employ it to her preference. This is important. The purpose of disputing is twofold: not only are you encouraging your client to relinquish her irrational beliefs, you are also encouraging her to 'embrace' her rational beliefs. Helping her to see that her rational beliefs are consistent with reality, logical and useful is a part of this process. So, note that I apply the main arguments to both Linda's irrational belief and her rational belief.]

Linda: It's consistent with reality.
Windy: Because?
Linda: Because while it shows what I don't want to happen, it points to the fact that I may cause Gill to binge. It recognizes that there is no law preventing it from happening.
Windy: Good. That's what we call empirical disputing of your demand. We check whether or not your demand is consistent or inconsistent with reality. And we use the same check on your preference belief. Now, a second way of evaluating your demand is to see if it follows logically from your preference belief. So we know that you don't want to cause Gill to binge, but does it logically follow that therefore you must not do so?

[I am now applying the logical argument to Linda's demand.]

Linda: Well, I guess not.

[It is important that you pay close attention to what your client says and how she says it. This is particularly important during the disputing process where phrases like 'I guess not' or 'I suppose so' are indicative of client doubt about the point under consideration. The best thing that you can do in these circumstances is to address this possible doubt immediately and directly as I do below.]

Windy: You don't sound too sure.
Linda: I guess I'm not.

[Linda's response indicates that I need to address the issue of the logicality of her demand in a different way.]

Windy: Well, look at it this way. Do you play the lottery?
Linda: Yes.
Windy: Would you like to win the jackpot?
Linda: Of course I would.
Windy: Is it logical then for you to conclude that because you want to win the lottery therefore you have to do so?
Linda: Of course not

[Here, as elsewhere, it is important to encourage your client to understand why her belief is irrational and not just that it is irrational. So, I ask Linda to explain why her demand is illogical.]

Windy: Why not?
Linda: Because what I want has no logical connection with what will happen.
Windy: Right. Your demand that you must not cause Gill to binge does not logically follow from your desire not to do so. But your desire is perfectly sensible, isn't it?

[Note again that I apply the logical argument to Linda's preference as well as to her demand.]

Linda: On its own, yes.
Windy: That is a really good point. On its own your desire is sensible; the illogicality comes in when you say: 'Because I don't want this to happen, therefore it must not.' Do you see that?
Linda: Yes, I do.
Windy: So that's what we call evaluating your demand along logical lines — and your desire, too. Now, the final way of evaluating your demand is along pragmatic lines. Now, what are the consequences for you when you demand that you absolutely must not cause Gill to go off on a binge?

[Having finished disputing Linda's demand with respect to its logicality, I finally move on to disputing it on pragmatic grounds.]

Linda: I'd feel terribly guilty if I do actually cause her to binge . . .
Windy: Right . . .
Linda: And if I believe this then I won't be prepared even to attempt
           to set healthy limits with Gill, because I would be so scared
           that she would be upset even in response to my most gentle
           approach.
Windy: That's an excellent point, with the result that you will spend
           many hours helping her and, probably — we don't know for
           sure — but probably increasing her dependency on you. And
           would that be good for her or for you?
Linda: Most certainly not!

[Linda clearly sees that her demand yields poor emotional and behavioural results. So, I move on by applying the pragmatic criterion to her
preference.]

Windy: Right. Now, let's employ the same pragmatic argument to
           your desire. What will be the likely consequences for you if
           you believe: 'I really don't want to cause Gill to go out and
           binge, but unfortunately there is no law of the universe for-
           bidding this from happening?'
Linda: Well, I would feel . . . what word did you call it? Oh, yes. I
           would feel remorse.
Windy: And would this belief stop you from setting healthy limits with
           Gill?
Linda: No, it wouldn't. I'd still feel concerned as I went about doing
           it, but, no, it wouldn't stop me.
Windy: That's right, it wouldn't stop you. In fact, it would encourage
           you to go carefully and probably reduce, but not eradicate,
           the risk that Gill will take what you say in a disturbed way.
           Can you see that?
Linda: Yes, I can.

[Linda can see clearly that her preference has healthier results than her
demand. Consequently, I decide to recap on the entire disputing
sequence that I have carried out with respect to Linda's demand.]

Windy: So let's just recap on the work that we have just done. We've
           been helping you to re-evaluate the demand that is at the core
           of your avoidance and guilt. We've been using three criteria.
           Basically, is your demand that you must not cause Gill's binge
           consistent with reality? Is it logical? And does it bring about
           healthy results? And we concluded . . . ?
Linda: That my belief is not consistent with reality, that it is illogical
           and that it tends to bring about unhealthy results.

Windy: And what did we conclude about your preference belief, namely: 'I would much prefer not to cause Gill's binge, but there is no law of the universe that states that I absolutely should not do so'?

Linda: That it is consistent with reality, logical and leads to healthier results.

Windy: At this point, you understand that your demand is self-defeating and your preference is healthier. Right?

Linda: Right.

Windy: Now, while this understanding is very important, on its own it won't necessarily help you set healthy limits with Gill and if you do manage to do this, this understanding won't on its own help you to feel remorse should you actually cause Gill to binge. Do you know why?

[Here I introduce Linda to the idea that while understanding that her demand is irrational and her preference is rational is important, it will not, on its own, help her to deepen her conviction in her rational belief (Sequence: Step 10).]

Linda: While I can see these things, I don't truly believe them.

Windy: Exactly. That's a very good insight. Now, while I can't help you to deepen your conviction in your preference belief and weaken your conviction in your demand in this one session, I will at the end give you some suggestions on how you can do this for yourself and, if you want to follow this up in ongoing therapy, as I said at the outset we can help set this up for you.

Linda: Fine.

[Having established for Linda the parameters of a demonstration session with respect to deepening her conviction in her preference, I proceed to dispute her self-downing derivative from her demand. In doing so, note that I use the same structure that I employed in disputing her demand; namely, by employing empirical, logical and pragmatic arguments.]

Windy: But first I want us to consider the second part of your belief. Now, if I recall, your full belief was: 'I absolutely must not cause Gill to go off on a binge and if I do this wrong thing, then I am a bad person.' Is that right?

Linda: Yes, that's right.

Windy: So, let's take the second part of that belief, namely: 'I am a bad person if I do the wrong thing and cause Gill to go off and binge.' Now, remember we are still assuming that you can, in fact, cause Gill to go off and binge and that that is the wrong thing to do. Now, is it true that you are a bad person if you do this bad thing?

[Once again, I remind Linda that we are still assuming that her inferences at A are true. Also, note my use of Socratic questioning in the following disputing sequence.]

Linda: Well, I wouldn't be a bad person if I didn't do it.
Windy: But does doing this bad thing make you a bad person?
Linda: I guess not.
Windy: Why not?
Linda: I'm not sure.
Windy: Well, if you were a bad person through and through, what type of things could you only do?
Linda: Bad things?
Windy: That's right. Now, have you heard the phrase 'fallible human being'?
Linda: Yes.
Windy: What does it mean?
Linda: It means that you can make errors.
Windy: Right, it means that you can do bad things, good things and neutral things. Now, we have agreed that causing Gill to go off and binge is bad. But does that prove you are a bad person through and through or does it prove that you are a fallible human being who has done the wrong thing?
Linda: It proves that I'm fallible. But isn't that a cop-out?

[Here Linda voices a common objection to the value of self-acceptance for wrongdoings.]

Windy: What do you mean?
Linda: Well, doesn't saying: 'I'm a fallible human being' mean that I am excusing myself?
Windy: No, not at all. When you accept yourself as a fallible human being who has done the wrong thing, you are still acknowledging that you have done the wrong thing and you take full responsibility for your actions. In fact, accepting yourself in this way helps you to think carefully about reasons for your behaviour and to learn from the experience in future. Have you found that blaming or condemning yourself for your actions has helped you to think objectively about your behaviour and to learn from it?

[In responding to Linda's objection, I briefly adopt a didactic style, but note that I end my response with a question designed to involve Linda in the process. Also note that I am addressing the question of the utility of self-acceptance versus self-blame. This, of course, addresses the pragmatic nature of the two beliefs.]

Linda: No, putting it like that, I haven't found that at all. In fact, blaming myself has meant that I have been wrapped up entirely with my own guilt feelings.

Windy: And can you think objectively about the reasons for your behaviour when you are in the midst of guilt?

Linda: No. When I'm feeling guilty, I'm anything but objective. In fact, when I feel guilty I think only that things are my fault.

Windy: Precisely. So accepting yourself as a fallible human being achieves two things. It encourages you to take responsibility for your actions and helps you to think about your behaviour objectively and learn from it. So, can you see that telling yourself that you are a bad person is not only inconsistent with reality, but it will give you lousy results?

Linda: Yes, I can see that very clearly.

Windy: And can you also see that accepting yourself as a fallible human being while taking responsibility for your behaviour is true and more likely to give you sounder, healthier results?

Linda: Yes, you've persuaded me that that's the case.

[Having dealt with the pragmatic nature of the two beliefs, I move on to the question of their logical status. Note that when I disputed Linda's demand I used empirical, logical and pragmatic questions in that order, whereas while disputing her self-downing belief, I used a different order, i.e. empirical, pragmatic and logical. The latter order was dictated mainly by Linda's concern that self-acceptance was a cop-out. The point I wish to stress here is that there is no set order for using the three types of argument. What is important is that you remain with a line of questioning until your client has grasped the point you are making. Avoid confusing your client by switching among the three types of argument.]

Windy: So, one more question to go. Is it good logic to say that because you have done the wrong thing, therefore you are a bad person?

Linda: I'm not sure I know what you mean.

Windy: Well, we're assuming that you have caused Gill to go out and binge and that that is a bad thing to do. Right?

Linda: Right.

Windy: And would you agree that that one act is only a tiny fragment of your whole being?

Linda: Yes, I would.

Windy: Well, is it good logic to say that that small part of you makes
          the whole of you bad?
Linda: No, it certainly doesn't.
Windy: Right, that would be making the part–whole error, where you
          define the whole of something on the basis of a part of it. But
          is it logical to conclude that you are fallible human being — a
          mixture of good, bad and neutral aspects — for acting badly
          by making Gill go out and binge?
Linda: Yes, that is logical.
Windy: So, let's recap on the work that we have done on the second
          part of your belief, which was that you would be a bad person
          if you caused Gill to go out and binge. Again, we looked at
          that belief in terms of whether it is consistent with reality, log-
          ical and functional. And what did we conclude?

[Once again I summarize the work we have done disputing Linda's self-
downing belief.]

Linda: That it was none of those things, but that the alternative belief
          where I accept myself as a fallible human for having done the
          wrong thing is true, logical and . . . what was the last thing?
Windy: Functional . . .
Linda: Functional . . . that it will give me better results.
Windy: Now, remember what I said earlier. Just knowing all this isn't
          enough. You need to really believe it. Now, let me give you
          two suggestions concerning how you can weaken your con-
          viction in your unhealthy belief and deepen your conviction
          in the healthy alternative. OK?

[Once again, I prepare Linda for the process of deepening her conviction in her rational belief and ask her if she is interested in two ways of
promoting this process (Sequence: Step 10).]

Linda: I'm all ears.
Windy: Now, the first thing that you can do is take the healthy belief:
          'I really would prefer not to have caused Gill to go on a binge,
          but unfortunately there is no law of the universe to say that I
          must not do so. If I do so, then I can still accept myself as a
          fallible human being who has done a very wrong thing.' Then
          write it down on a piece of paper. Second, rate how much
          you really believe it on a scale of 0–100%. Third, write down
          something that attacks that belief using any argument that
          occurs to you. Fourth, respond to this attack with a plausible
          argument, ripping it up. Proceed in this way until you have
          responded to all the attacks you can think of and then re-rate

your conviction in the original healthy belief you started with. If you do the exercise properly you should increase your conviction in the new, healthy belief. Is that clear?

[The technique that I have described to Linda is called the zig-zag technique. It is described more fully in another volume in this series, which describes therapeutic techniques commonly used in REBT (Dryden and Yankura, forthcoming). Due to the limitation of time remaining in this demonstration interview, I am fairly rushed in my explanation, but, as you will see, I do give Linda written instructions on how to use the zig-zag technique. In a regular therapy session, I would go much more slowly in teaching my client how to use this technique and would spend more time discussing its use as a possible homework assignment (see Sequence: Step 11).]

Linda: Yes, but it is a lot to take in in one go.
Windy: Right, so I'll give you a written list of these instructions at the end of the session.
Linda: Oh, good.
Windy: Now, a second way of increasing your conviction in the healthy belief is to act on it. You may not want to do so immediately with Gill. But can you think of a less challenging example where you can assert yourself and practise the new belief before, during and after doing so?

[The zig-zag technique that I have just described to Linda is predominantly a cognitive technique. I also want to stress to Linda that a powerful way of deepening her conviction in her rational belief is to act on that belief. I am of the opinion, however, that it is too early for Linda to do so with her sister. On reflection, it would have been better for me to test this out with Linda rather than assuming unilaterally that this was the case. In any event, I did act unilaterally on this point and ask Linda if she can think of a less challenging example where she can practise her new rational belief while acting on that new belief (by asserting herself). As you will see, Linda does identify such an example and I help her to prepare for this in the session by encouraging her to rehearse her new beliefs at important junctures in this imagined scenario. Notice my use of questions in this process.]

Linda: . . . Yes, I can think of something.
Windy: Tell me.
Linda: Well, I have a friend that I find it hard to say no to. So, the next time she asks me for a favour, I can refuse to do it.
Windy: Now, the important thing about doing this, which we call a behavioural exercise, is that you practise your new belief

	while doing so. So what will you tell yourself before you turn her down?
Linda:	Well, I can remind myself that I have a right to say no . . .
Windy:	. . . And if you, so to speak, hurt her feelings?
Linda:	Well, I wouldn't like it, but I can accept myself for doing so. There's no law to prevent me from hurting her feelings. But I'm not doing so maliciously.
Windy:	Right. And you can rehearse this belief after the fact, too, whether or not you, in quotes, 'hurt her feelings'. Now, do you think that doing this would be good preparation for what you need to say to your sister?
Linda:	Yes, that would help a lot.
Windy:	So will you agree to assert yourself with your friend?
Linda:	Yes, I will.

[Having agreed with Linda that she will take this behavioural task as a homework assignment (Sequence: Step 11), I have one remaining task to accomplish. You will recall that throughout the assessment and disputing sequences, I have encouraged Linda to assume temporarily that her inferences at A were correct. This is a defining feature of REBT and its purpose is to encourage the client to identify and challenge the irrational beliefs that underlie her inferences. Once the client has done this, she is in a more objective frame of mind to evaluate her inferences. So, my final task in this session is to encourage Linda to question her inferences, in particular that if Gill, in response to Linda's limit-setting, goes off on a binge that Linda can be said directly to cause her sister's behaviour. Note that I give Linda a rationale for this ordering of interventions before disputing her inference.]

Windy:	Now, there is one more issue that I want to raise with you before we finish. OK?
Linda:	Hm-hmm.
Windy:	Throughout this interview we have accepted your point that you can, in fact, cause Gill to go off and binge. Now, the reason I have taken this tack is because it has let us identify the beliefs that are at the core of your guilt and which help prevent you from asserting yourself with Gill. In my book, *Overcoming Guilt* (Dryden, 1994), I suggest that whenever you feel guilty about doing something, for example, you assume temporarily that you did, in fact, do it, that it was bad and that you are responsible for doing it. Then you identify and challenge the ideas that are at the core of your guilt. Once you have done this then you are likely to be in a better frame of mind to consider objectively whether or not you can be said to cause Gill to go off and binge if she does so after

Linda: you have set limits with her. You can't easily do this when you are feeling guilty. Am I making myself clear?

Linda: I think so.

Windy: Can you put that into your own words?

[Whenever you have didactically explained a substantial point to your client, it is useful to check her understanding of this point.]

Linda: You're saying that when you feel guilt it is important to assume for the moment that you have done something wrong. And you wait until you have found and questioned your beliefs before looking at whether or not you are to blame.

Windy: Excellent, although I would say whether you are responsible, rather than to blame.

Linda: I see.

Windy: Now, let's suppose that you do lay down clear boundaries with Gill and let's suppose that she does go off and binge. Who is responsible for what?

Linda: Well, I guess it depends on how I say it to her.

Windy: That's a good point. If you set limits in a hostile way, you do increase the chances that Gill will go on a binge, but even here can you be said to cause her behaviour?

Linda: I guess not.

Windy: Why not?

Linda: Because, theoretically anyway, it is her beliefs about what I said that would lead her to binge.

Windy: Why theoretically?

Linda: Because I know Gill and if I was hostile to her, she would definitely go out and binge. She'll probably do so even if I am nice.

Windy: But does that mean that you cause her behaviour or that she very easily causes her own behaviour?

Linda: That she easily causes her own behaviour.

Windy: Now, because she is so vulnerable, you will need to take extra care in what you say to her. Right?

Linda: Right.

Windy: But, if you do take care and she goes off on a binge, who is primarily responsible for this?

Linda: She is.

[Note that up to now I have adopted a Socratic style of questioning. I now underscore the point didactically.]

Windy: Right, you are responsible for what you know about Gill and for how you address the issue of limit-setting with her. But she is responsible for her beliefs, her feelings and her behaviour. The fact that she is basically responsible for going on a binge doesn't give you *carte blanche* over how you treat her. But it does mean that if you set limits in a sensitive way and she responds by going on a binge, she is basically responsible for doing so. Can you see that?

Linda: Yes. But I'll still feel badly if she does so.

Windy: Right, it's healthy to feel concerned about such a possibility. Now, before we close let me stress that in order to get over your guilt and avoidance, assume temporarily that you did cause Gill's binge and after you've done that remind yourself about who is responsible for what in the event of her binge. OK?

[Once again, I stress the typical REBT sequencing of interventions on this issue.]

Linda: OK.
Windy: Good luck with saying no to your friend.
Linda: Thanks.
Windy: And thank you for coming here today.
Linda: Thank you for your help.

[You will note that I did not cover Step 5 of the REBT treatment sequence in my interview with Linda, i.e. Identify and assess any meta-emotional problems. The reason for this was twofold. First, assessing Linda's target C was somewhat difficult as there were two candidates: anxiety and guilt. To then introduce the concept of a meta-emotional problem would, in my opinion, have been too confusing for Linda. Second, my clinical hunch was that Linda did not have a meta-emotional problem about her guilt or, if she did have one, it would have less significance than her guilt. I could have checked this out and in a regular non-demonstration session I probably would have done so. I considered that had I done so here, I would have run the risk of losing the momentum that I had developed at that point of the interview and, as noted above, Linda could well have become confused as a result. Let me stress, however, that its omission in this interview does not signifying its lack of importance in the REBT treatment sequence.]

Chapter 5
Transcript of Demonstration Session II. Therapist: Albert Ellis

In this chapter, I provide a transcript of a demonstration session conducted by Albert Ellis with a volunteer from the cohort of trainees on an introductory REBT training course. This interview was conducted towards the end of the course, so Susan, the trainee, will have learned about the basics of REBT theory and practice and will have had an opportunity to practise REBT in peer counselling sessions. As Susan understands something about REBT and will have been taught the ABCs of REBT (unlike Linda in the previous demonstration session, who knew very little about REBT), Albert Ellis probably takes this into account and explains less about REBT than he would do if Susan knew nothing about this approach to therapy.

Once again, trainees will have agreed to treat in confidence the material discussed by trainee volunteers and the latter will have given their permission for the interview to be taped for later professional use.

I again suggest that you keep in mind the REBT treatment sequence presented in Chapter 2 while reading and studying the transcript of Albert Ellis' interview with Susan as it was conducted.

The Interview

Albert: OK, what problem would you like to raise?

Susan: I'd like to raise something that was raised yesterday, that I thought I had, er, completely overcome.

Albert: Yeah, what was that?

Susan: Well, it was pointed out to me, that I said, er: 'Well I don't torture myself any more.' I mean, that was 20 years ago I tortured myself, no more, and two of the young men in the room said: 'Is that so? Because 20 minutes ago [laughing], you know, I heard you torturing yourself.'

91

Albert: Yeah.

Susan: And I thought, wow, you know. Right, I just do it in smaller bits now. I used to do it globally and, er . . .

Albert: And they picked that up that you were still torturing yourself.

Susan: Right. And that . . . er . . . I was very disappointed.

Albert: Because you thought that you had ended that sort of thing?

Susan: I thought I had conquered that.

Albert: And they sort of brought to your attention again that you're still torturing yourself. And in what way would you say you're mainly torturing yourself now that you're looking at it?

Susan: Well, what brought it up, er . . . yesterday, was this . . . this whole practicum. Er . . . that I'm very . . . [sighing], I'm very disturbed by the fact that I don't think I do it well, that when I do the sessions with one partner that, you know, I just seem to be either floating round in the air or . . . or blocking, and everybody else seems to be doing so well. And this was the basis of the torture.

Albert: So, first you *see* that they're doing better than you, you're not doing that well, and then you torture yourself, if I understand you correctly, *about* seeing that. Is that right?

Susan: Yes, er . . . but as you say, first you see I . . . I realise . . . something clicks in, and I'm evaluating it that way, I'm perceiving it that way, it doesn't necessarily have to *be* that way.

Albert: Right. But you could perceive it and evaluate it differently. But first let's assume, because you may be exaggerating, you may *not* be doing *that* poorly, but let's just assume for the sake of discussion that what you're seeing, your perception, is accurate. You *are* doing poorly. Then, how do you torture yourself about that? What is your evaluation, as you just sort of indicated?

Susan: I don't know if I would say that I torture myself. I think I, er . . . more or less begin to say: 'Well this isn't so important anyhow and I guess I really don't wanna do this *really*, it's just taking up a week of time and that's great. It's interesting but, er . . . you know, it's not that important.'

Albert: So, we would call that withdrawal? You sort of withdraw from the situation, and view it as not very important, is that right?

Susan: Yeah.

Albert: But do you think that *underneath* that view, that 'I'm finding this not important', you're first sort of torturing yourself and therefore withdrawing. Is that your view of the torture?

Susan: I don't know, I'm not really, er . . . yeah . . . yeah.

Albert: Do you think that may be going on?

Susan: I'm having a little trouble with defining torture.

Albert: All right. But we can even skip torture, because we can just look at what we call C, the consequence, which would be withdrawal. So, at A, the activating event in our system of Rational Emotive Behaviour Therapy, you're perceiving that you're not doing well and we're assuming, you and I, that that's true — that may be false, but let's assume that's true — and then at C, you withdraw, maybe defensively. Is that right?

Susan: Yes.

Albert: That maybe you're withdrawing defensively, but at least you withdraw. Now, what do you think you're telling yourself at B, to cause that withdrawal?

Susan: OK, umm, 'I'm not as bright as I think I am', er . . . 'these guys are really far more well-trained than . . . I am', umm, 'They're more perceptive than I am', 'I really have no perception . . . I don't know what the hell I'm doing', er . . . 'I can't even drag out of a session the kernel of the problem, and if I'm lucky enough to happen on the kernel of the problem, *what do I do*?' You know, er, I'm er . . . I don't know what to do, I don't feel schooled, or trained, or . . . or able, umm, to *be* a therapist.

Albert: Right. Those are all observations that you're making about your performance compared with their performance. 'I'm not bright enough', 'I'm not well-schooled enough', 'I seem to be confused about what to do'; is that right?

Susan: Yes.

Albert: You're observing those things about your performance compared with *their* performance.

Susan: Well, I thought I was feeling those things.

Albert: Well, but at first; isn't there an observation that that's what you see? We'll get to the feeling in a minute, and we know the behaviour to a certain degree already: you're withdrawing. But once you perceive those things, and let's just assume the worst — we like to assume the worst in REBT just to show people that they can go with even the worst — so, let's assume you're accurate, you're quite accurate, that compared with them you are below par and that as a therapist compared with them again you're not so hot. That's what you're perceiving and evaluating, you're right, you are evaluating that. But *that* kind of observation and evaluation of performance wouldn't make you withdraw. Do you know why it wouldn't make you withdraw if you only stuck with that kind of observation and evaluation: why wouldn't you withdraw?

Susan: Possibly because I see others who are equally inept.

Albert: That would be one thing. That's right. You see others who are inept. But also you could conclude: 'Even though this is so, I'm glad I now see that. Maybe I'd better throw myself into it more and get more training and overcome these deficiencies.' Couldn't that be a legitimate conclusion?

Susan: Yes . . . yes.

Albert: And then you wouldn't withdraw.

Susan: Right.

Albert: But we know that you *did* feel like withdrawing. Right?

Susan: Yes.

Albert: That's your feeling: 'I don't wanna be here. I'd better with-draw.' Now, therefore, we believe in REBT that there's an additional evaluation. In addition to the evaluation of your performance, you're saying something *stronger* about *it* and about *you*. Now, if I'm right about that, and I could be wrong but I'm just hypothesizing now, what would you be saying that's *stronger* that would make you withdraw?

Susan: If I continue I'm gonna make a real ass of myself.

Albert: And if I make an ass of myself . . .

Susan: If I make a real ass of myself [laughing], it's another notch in my belt of asshood.

Albert: Right. And that proves *what* about you?

Susan: That I will die an ass.

Albert: I will *always* be an ass, I'm a hopeless ass do you mean, or something like that?

Susan: I am never going to er . . . I am never going to get it all straightened out.

Albert: Right. Now, do you see then, that you have two sets of obser-vations and evaluations? The first one, merely 'Compared with them I'm not doing well, and maybe I never will.' And that *might* be true, you see. It could be that you're just evaluating correctly, that your performance is never going to be up to theirs. But *then* you say: 'My performance makes me an ass and a hopeless ass and I'll *die* an ass as I *live* an ass,' is that right?

Susan: Yes.

Albert: Now *that's* the evaluation . . .

Susan: [Laughing] My God, that sounds terrible.

Albert: That's right, you see. And that's what we want to question, and that's why we go to D, disputing. Let's suppose the worst again, that your observation is true and let's even suppose you go *on* acting this way, you're not very good at therapy as they are. How does that make *you*, a human, an ass?

Susan: I guess somewhere I feel that I *have to* excel at *something*.

Albert: Right. You see the '*have to*'.

Susan: I *have to* excel at something.

Albert: And if you change that '*have to*', to 'I'd *like* to excel at something, but if I don't, I don't', would you then feel like an ass?

Susan: No, I wouldn't. But I really *have* to change the whole statement anyway. I *have* to excel at *everything*. I want to excel at *everything* I touch.

Albert: Well, but you notice you just said two things. I *want to* excel at everything', which I think almost every human says, 'I'd *like to*', 'I *want to* excel at all *important* things'. Not tiddly-winks, you don't care if you don't excel at tiddly-winks, do you?

Susan: No, that would be all right. *That* would show that I was only human.

Albert: Yes, right. But you want to excel at every important thing and then you say 'and therefore I *have to*', is that right?

Susan: Yes.

Albert: Now, in REBT we never question desires, preferences, wishes, wants, because you could *want* anything. You could want, right now, 10 million dollars, or to be the greatest genius at therapy in the world, and as long as you were saying 'I *want* it, but 'I don't *have to*', you wouldn't be into trouble. But we question the '*have to*'. Why *must* you excel at an important thing like therapy? Why must you?

Susan: I don't know.

Albert: Well, think about that.

Susan: Well, I dunno. I suppose . . . er . . . I think it may be that I'm a product of growing up where I've been told, or it's been implied that if you do something, do it well.

Albert: Right. Let's suppose that's true. And, incidentally, that has sense to it, because if you do something well, it would be *preferable* to doing it poorly. We all learn that because that's not false. Our parents and our schools and our books teach us to 'try to do well. If at once you don't succeed, try, try again to succeed.' Isn't that what it means? And so that's OK. But we're still asking another question, not why it's *preferable* to do well, why *must* you do what's preferable? Why do you *have to*?

Susan: I feel better when I . . . when I *do* accomplish. I feel better about myself.

Albert: Ah, about *yourself*. But you see you've just again said two things, (1) 'I feel better about *it*,' which we hope is true — that you would feel better about accomplishment rather than sitting on your rump and doing nothing or doing badly. So you'd better feel better about it. But you're saying 'I feel better about *me*, I only accept *me* when I do *it* well.' Now, is *that* a legitimate conclusion? 'I can only accept *me*, *myself*, my *being*, my totality, when I do *it*, therapy, well.' Now is that a good conclusion?

Susan: You mean, is it accurate?

Albert: Well, will it give you good results?

Susan: No, it won't give me good results.

Albert: It'll give you what you have . . . withdrawal, anxiety. Maybe what you said at the beginning of this session, some kind of anguish, terror almost, which may be the thing that is making you withdraw — which we could just guess about, but it certainly *won't give you pleasure* and it won't help you to stay with this practicum or any other thing that you enter. You'll tend to run away. And by running away will you do as well as you'd like to do?

Susan: No.

Albert: You'll normally do worse, isn't that so?

Susan: Well, I will not have accomplished anything at all.

Albert: That's right.

Susan: Except to have reinforced again, once again, Susan strikes out.

Albert: That's the irony, you see. That's really an irony. By demanding that 'I must do "X" well', such as therapy in a practicum. 'I *have to*', 'I *have to*', 'I've *got to*', 'I've *got to* do it *well*', you will *withdraw* and not even do it *at all*. You see the *need*, the *necessity* of, performing well leads to withdrawal or anxiety, which interferes with your performance. You see that's catch 22. Now, how do you think you can get out of that bind?

Susan: By not withdrawing and not being anxious.

Albert: That's right. First, not withdrawing. Then you still would be anxious if you didn't withdraw. Now, how could you get rid of your anxiety? Let's assume you stayed with it, and it was *uncomfortable* to stay. And that's what we recommend in REBT, to stay with your discomfort until you make yourself comfortable. *How* could you get rid of the anxiety by staying with your discomfort?

Susan: By applying myself more, and er . . . learning the techniques.

Albert: Right. That's one way, but that's a little inelegant. That would work, because let's suppose that you stayed with it no matter how uncomfortable you felt and you learned the techniques of doing therapy. You got better at it and you felt *unanxious*. Do you realize why that would be an inelegant kind of solution? It would work, temporarily, but why would it only work temporarily? Why would it be inelegant?

Susan: Because I think it attacks just a very small piece of it.

Albert: That's right. And even in that small piece, suppose you first did well, and then later did badly. Suppose you finished the practicum, learned REBT quite well, as well as anybody does, and then compare yourself with other therapists and *still* do poorly. Then what would you go back to telling yourself?

Susan: That I really don't belong here. I'll go back to the same thing.

Albert: And 'I'm a no-good person for being a no-good therapist.' You see, you haven't got rid of that. So the technique in REBT is, first, *stay* with the uncomfortable situation and then *work* on the anxiety by giving up your *must*. Now, how could you give up, 'I *must* do well', 'I *have to*', 'I've *got to*'?

Susan: By telling myself, 'OK, I will continue, and I will try, and I will do my best, and if it works out, that will be very nice. And if it doesn't work out, well maybe I'll try another kind of er . . . training.'

Albert: Or . . . 'Maybe I'll . . .'

Susan: I'll go into another field.

Albert: No, no . . . that's OK. Those are OK *practical* solutions. But better yet, 'Maybe I'll stay in this field and not *have* to be so great. It doesn't *have* to work out well — I don't *have* to do as well as the others.' Isn't that better?

Susan: Yes. I can be a student, a C student, and survive.

Albert: I often talk about the Sunday painters. They're out in the park with their easels and their paints every Sunday, painting some of the most *god-awful* things, and some of them know it and they *still* enjoy painting. Now how do they *continue* to paint those *god-awful* things and still enjoy it? What are they telling themselves?

Susan: One . . . they *like* those god-awful things.

Albert: Right.

Susan: And two, there's nothing wrong with those god-awful things.

Albert: Or better — there's nothing wrong with *them* for painting god-awfully. You see. And they even might say 'I don't like my paintings, but I like the *painting*.' They're doing poorly at the activity but allowing themselves to *enjoy* it. I always quote the statement of Oscar Wilde, 'Anything that's worth doing is worth doing *badly*.' You see? Because the *activity itself* is worth it. The *results* may *not* be worth it. You may never like the *results*. Now, as a therapist, we wouldn't want you to go on being a really bad therapist. And, as you said before, 'Maybe I'd better get into another field or something like that.' But that would be later when you've really determined that you're bad at therapy. First, you stay with your discomfort, as I said. Then you recognize that you are *creating* much of it. You *make* yourself anxious. Third, you see that you mainly do it by your '*have to*', your '*got to*', your '*must*'. And by 'I am a rotten person if I do badly, rottenly.' Then you *dispute*: 'Where is the evidence that I'm a rotten person or that I *have* to do well'? And what conclusion do you end up with then?

Susan: I'm beginning to wonder, am I really saying that I am a rotten person or am I really and truly saying, I am a rotten therapist?

Albert: Well, let's suppose you were. Let's suppose *that* for the moment. That would be . . . that might be sane. If you had enough evidence, if you did poorly time and again, and if you're not that good at therapy and you're concluding 'I am *rotten* at *therapy* and I'll never be more than average or mediocre at therapy', then that would be OK. But I doubt whether you'd withdraw from doing therapy so *quickly* if that were *so*.

Susan: Aaaah.

Albert: You see?

Susan: Aaaah.

Albert: Do you really have evidence?

Susan: I was going to say, I really needed evidence. I see. That I can understand.

Albert: You see, just like those Sunday painters. They might go week after week, 52 weeks of the year, to the park and paint, and then finally say, 'You know, I like the painting but I don't like the result. Maybe I'd better do sculpture. I would get better results.' That would be OK. But if they quit after the first week then we get suspicious of their self-downing. How do they even know they're right about their *painting* but not about *themselves* being no good? You see?

Susan: I know you might find it very difficult to believe, but at home I have now sitting umm . . . some paint and some canvases [laughing]. Because my daughter is getting me ready for retirement. She said, 'Gee, you've always said you'd like to paint.' I have not touched the paints for two months because . . . why? Because I know when I get to it the painting's gonna be lousy.

Albert: And it *should* right from the start be great?

Susan: Be terrific! Right.

Albert: Now isn't *that* something you're imposing on yourself? And you see it was interesting that I used painting as an example, and now it turns out that you're really in the position of copping out. But that's a good thing, because in therapy you'd at least have the excuse. 'Well if I'm rotten at therapy, I'd better not be a therapist because I might harm others.' Or something like that. But in painting, *who would you harm*? If you really work for weeks and months at it and it turned out that you were no good at it, who would be harmed? Would anybody be harmed?

Susan: No.

Albert: And you would have *learned* at least the valuable information that, 'You know, painting may not *be* my cup of tea.' You would have *gathered* some evidence. Now, in cases like yours, you're withdrawing too *quickly* and therefore we probably could call it defensive. But don't accept that you are defensive because I think you are or some other therapists think you are. We could be *wrong*. You might be very perceptive and sense quickly that you're not that good at therapy and decide to do something else. That would be legitimate. But *get the evidence*. You see? And the quicker you withdraw from doing therapy, the less evidence you'll have, you see?

Susan: Yeah, that's er . . .

Albert: Anything else you wanted to raise about this?

Susan: No . . . I think that . . . er, this is something I really have to, er . . . give a lot of thought to. Because it's, er . . . I . . . [sighing] I think this is the first time I feel that I'm down to the kernel. And, er . . . and I *could* do as I have done all these years, say, 'OK, terrific, that was a great session', and go out and have lunch and forget about it. But I'm gonna make myself sit on that kernel and chew on that kernel.

Albert: That's right . . .

Susan: . . . And unfold. Try to unfold.

Albert: And that's a very good point you're making. *Don't* assume that what I said was correct because I said it or because I have some status. See whether it applies to you and test it out, keep testing, you see.

Susan: Yeah. Uh-hum. [Bell rings] Was that the end?

Albert: No. That just happened to be the bell to open the door downstairs.

Susan: Because I feel very well satisfied that I have gotten quite a . . . quite a jolt here.

Albert: Now, how can you *use* that jolt to your benefit? That's the main thing.

Susan: [Sighing]. Well, I think what I'm gonna do is sit down at home and go over the past year or so of events where I have tried to do something and er . . . they have not worked out, . . . none of them has worked out and see whether indeed they have not worked out because I realistically evaluated it *or* er . . . I didn't give it enough time.

Albert: Withdrew too quickly. Right.

Susan: Which was something that was brought up yesterday too er . . . or, if . . . Have I given the things I have turned my hand to enough time and effort?

Albert: Right. That's a good point.

Susan: Because in my case there was plenty of time, but I don't know how much effort went into these activities.

Albert: Yeah. Because if you're telling yourself what we said before, let's just assume we're right, 'I *must* do well and isn't it awful if I don't.' And, 'If not, I might be a rotten therapist or even a rotten person.' If so, you may force yourself to continue at therapy and not really give it your *all*. So, the test of whether you're good at *anything* is: (1) take enough time, don't withdraw, and then (2) really throw yourself in and take it as a *challenge* to learn. You see? If you really are bad at something you still have the challenge of doing better. It's an interesting puzzle to solve if you take that attitude. Like, people don't play tic-tac-toe because it's too easy. Some of them don't even play chequers because it is too easy, so they play chess, or Go, or some complicated game, *knowing* they're going to lose but it's a greater challenge. Now you . . . this is your life, let's see if you can take the *challenge* of finding out whether quitting therapy is a cop-out on your part, which we're not sure about yet, because it could be. Or whether you are quickly ascertaining whether therapy is not for you. But give it more time, give it more effort, stop *must*urbating about it and then we'll see.

Susan: Yeah. Fine.

Albert: You see now what you can do?

Susan: Yeah. That will be my homework.

Albert: Yes. That will be your homework. To *consider* what we've said and test it as a hypothesis. It's *only* a hypothesis, and see whether you can find evidence for either your appropriately getting out of a situation, or running out pell-mell *de-fen-sive-ly*.

Susan: Yeah. And even as I now think, as you're talking, of the events of the past year or two, it's amazing to me that my conclusions always were 'Well, I am not, I am *not*, I am *not*' and so I dropped all of those efforts. Because I thought, 'I am *not*.'

Albert: But you could have said, 'Maybe I am not.' Let's see.

Susan: Yeah.

Albert: Right?

Susan: Right.

Albert: OK. You work on that.

Susan: Fine. Very good.
Albert: All right?
Susan: Well, I appreciate that.

Chapter 6
Commentary on Albert Ellis's Demonstration Session

In this chapter, I will provide an ongoing commentary on the demonstration session that was presented in the previous chapter. As with my commentary on my session with Linda (see Chapter 4), I will use the REBT treatment sequence discussed in Chapter 2 as the framework for my obseravations. In addition, I also include Albert Ellis's comments on the interview (which will be presented before my own).

Interview and Commentary

Albert: OK, what problem would you like to raise?

[Windy: Note the problem-oriented way that Albert begins this demonstration session (Sequence: Step 1).]

Susan: I'd like to raise something that was raised yesterday, that I thought I had, er, completely overcome.
Albert: Yeah, what was that?
Susan: Well, it was pointed out to me, that I said, er: 'Well I don't torture myself any more.' I mean, that was 20 years ago I tortured myself, no more, and two of the young men in the room said: 'Is that so? Because 20 minutes ago [laughing], you know, I heard you torturing yourself.'
Albert: Yeah.
Susan: And I thought, wow, you know. Right, I just do it in smaller bits now. I used to do it globally and, er . . .
Albert: And they picked that up that you were still torturing yourself.
Susan: Right. And that . . . er . . . I was very disappointed.
Albert: Because you thought that you had ended that sort of thing?
Susan: I thought I had conquered that.

Albert: And they sort of brought to your attention again that you're still torturing yourself. And in what way would you say you're mainly torturing yourself now that you're looking at it?

[Windy: Albert intervenes to bring specificity to Susan's rather vague description of her problem (Sequence: Initiating Step 2).]

Susan: Well, what brought it up, er . . . yesterday, was this . . . this whole practicum. Er . . . that I'm very . . . [sighing], I'm very disturbed by the fact that I don't think I do it well, that when I do the sessions with one partner that, you know, I just seem to be either floating round in the air or . . . or blocking, and everybody else seems to be doing so well. And this was the basis of the torture.

Albert: So, first you *see* that they're doing better than you, you're not doing that well, and then you torture yourself, if I understand you correctly, *about* seeing that. Is that right?

[Windy: Here Albert is ensuring that he understands Susan's problem from her perspective (Sequence: Step 2).]

Susan: Yes, er . . . but as you say, first you see I . . . I realise . . . something clicks in, and I'm evaluating it that way, I'm perceiving it that way, it doesn't necessarily have to *be* that way.

Albert: Right. But you could perceive it and evaluate it differently. But first let's assume, because you may be exaggerating, you may *not* be doing *that* poorly, but let's just assume for the sake of discussion that what you're seeing, your perception, is accurate. You *are* doing poorly. Then, how do you torture yourself about that? What is your evaluation, as you just sort of indicated?

[Albert: I know I am only going to have this one session with this client, so I want to quickly, with her assent, determine the ABCs of her disturbance. I tentatively decide, at this point, that A is her perception of her doing poorly as a therapist in the practicum; B is her underlying demand, 'I must do better than this — and at least as good as the other therapists at this practicum. If I don't, I'm an incompetent therapist and something of an incompetent person (IP)!' C is her feelings of anxiety and depression. I sort of non-directively explore to see if my surmises about her ABCs are probably accurate.]

[Windy: Albert has done three things in this intervention. First, he distinguishes between perceptions (at A) and evaluations (at B). Second, he identifies Susan's A — that she is doing poorly and third, he adopts the typical REBT tack at this stage — assuming temporarily that her A is true (Sequence: Step 4). You will note that Albert identifies Susan's A a little before her C, but this is OK as there are no hard and fast rules concerning whether to assess C before A or vice versa.]

Susan: I don't know if I would say that I torture myself. I think I, er . . . more or less begin to say 'Well this isn't so important anyhow and I guess I really don't wanna do this *really*, it's just taking up a week of time and that's great. It's interesting but, er . . . you know, it's not that important.'
Albert: So, we would call that withdrawal? You sort of withdraw from the situation, and view it as not very important, is that right?
Susan: Yeah.

[Albert: I now have found a behavioural C — withdrawal; and perhaps a defensive philosophy; 'This situation is not very important — because if I viewed it as important, I would really have to put myself down for failing at it.']

[Windy: As Albert has just noted, he has identified her C, which in this instance is behavioural not emotional (Sequence: Step 3).]

Albert: But do you think that *underneath* that view, that 'I'm finding this not important', you're first sort of torturing yourself and therefore withdrawing. Is that your view of the torture?
Susan: I don't know, I'm not really, er . . . yeah . . . yeah.
Albert: Do you think that may be going on?
Susan: I'm having a little trouble with defining torture.
Albert: All right. But we can even skip torture, because we can just look at what we call C, the consequence, which would be withdrawal. So, at A, the activating event in our system of Rational Emotive Behaviour Therapy, you're perceiving that you're not doing well and we're assuming, you and I, that that's true — that may be false, but let's assume that's true — and then at C, you withdraw, maybe defensively. Is that right?
Susan: Yes.

[Albert: Although she agrees to the C of defensive withdrawal, I still hypothesize to myself that she is withdrawing from 'torture' — meaning anxiety, depression, self-damnation and feelings of severe inadequacy.]

[Windy: As Albert notes, by putting 'torture' in inverted commas, this term is very vague and probably encompasses B and C elements. As he notes above, 'torture' can be 'skipped' and her A and C elements can be formulated using more specific referents. Note also that in his above response Albert is specific in mentioning A and C. Because Susan is a participant on a primary REBT practicum, she will know what these letters refer to. Hence, he offers her no explanation.]

Albert: That maybe you're withdrawing defensively, but at least you withdraw. Now, what do you think you're telling yourself at B, to cause that withdrawal?

[Windy: Again, as Susan is a primary practicum participant she knows the iB-C connection (Sequence: Step 6). Thus, Albert goes straight to assessing her irrational beliefs (Sequence: Step 7). Note that he does so using open-ended rather than theory-driven questions (see pp. 34–35).]

Susan: OK, umm, 'I'm not as bright as I think I am', er . . . 'these guys are really far more well-trained than . . . I am', umm, 'They're more perceptive than I am', 'I really have no perception . . . I don't know what the hell I'm doing', er . . . 'I can't even drag out of a session the kernel of the problem, and if I'm lucky enough to happen on the kernel of the problem, *what do I do?*' You know, er, I'm er . . . I don't know what to do, I don't feel schooled, or trained, or . . . or able, umm, to *be* a therapist.

[Windy: Note that Susan does not offer irrational beliefs in response to Albert's open ended enquiry. Rather, she comes up with further inferences at A (or what in his next response Albert refers to as observations).]

Albert: Right. Those are all observations that you're making about your performance compared with their performance. 'I'm not bright enough', 'I'm not well-schooled enough', 'I seem to be confused about what to do'; is that right?
Susan: Yes.
Albert: You're observing those things about your performance compared with *their* performance.
Susan: Well, I thought I was feeling those things.
Albert: Well, but at first; isn't there an observation that that's what you see? We'll get to the feeling in a minute, and we know the behaviour to a certain degree already: you're withdrawing. But once you perceive those things, and let's just assume the worst — we like to assume the worst in REBT just to show people that they can go with even the worst — so, let's assume you're accurate, you're quite accurate, that compared with them you are below par and that as a therapist compared

with them again you're not so hot. That's what you're perceiving and evaluating, you're right, you are evaluating that. But *that* kind of observation and evaluation of performance wouldn't make you withdraw. Do you know why it wouldn't make you withdraw if you only stuck with that kind of observation and evaluation: why wouldn't you withdraw?

[Windy: Here Albert does a number of things. First, he helps Susan to distinguish between her perceptions (or what I call inferences) and her feelings. Second, he reminds Susan that they are still assuming that her A is true (Sequence: Reiterating Step 4). Finally, he distinguishes between perceptions and evaluations of performance (which properly belong at A) and a more central type of evaluation that explains her withdrawal and which constitutes irrational beliefs at B (as we shall soon see).]

Susan: Possibly because I see others who are equally inept.
Albert: That would be one thing. That's right. You see others who are inept. But also you could conclude: 'Even though this is so, I'm glad I now see that. Maybe I'd better throw myself into it more and get more training and overcome these deficiencies.' Couldn't that be a legitimate conclusion?
Susan: Yes . . . yes.
Albert: And then you wouldn't withdraw.
Susan: Right.
Albert: But we know that you *did* feel like withdrawing. Right?
Susan: Yes.
Albert: That's your feeling: 'I don't wanna be here. I'd better withdraw.' Now, therefore, we believe in REBT that there's an additional evaluation. In addition to the evaluation of your performance, you're saying something *stronger* about *it* and about *you*. Now, if I'm right about that, and I could be wrong but I'm just hypothesizing now, what would you be saying that's *stronger* that would make you withdraw?

[Windy: Again, Albert is adopting an open-ended rather than a theory-driven enquiry to help Susan discover her irrational beliefs at B (Sequence: Step 7).]

Susan: If I continue I'm gonna make a real ass of myself.
Albert: And if I make an ass of myself . . .
Susan: If I make a real ass of myself [laughing], it's another notch in my belt of asshood.
Albert: Right. And that proves *what* about you?
Susan: That I will die an ass.
Albert: I will *always* be an ass, I'm a hopeless ass do you mean, or something like that?

Susan: I am never going to er . . . I am never going to get it all
           straightened out.

Albert: Right. Now, do you see then, that you have two sets of obser-
           vations and evaluations ? The first one, merely 'Compared
           with them I'm not doing well, and maybe I never will.' And
           that *might* be true, you see. It could be that you're just evalu-
           ating correctly, that your performance is never going to be up
           to theirs. But *then* you say: 'My performance makes me an ass
           and a hopeless ass and I'll *die* an ass as I *live* an ass,' is that
           right?

[Windy: Here Albert helps Susan to discriminate keenly between her
self-downing irrational belief and her evaluation of performance at A.]

Susan: Yes.

[Albert: More and more she is confirming my inner assumptions about
her ABCs. Of course, she is a therapist and knows some REBT, so she
may be giving me the 'right' ABCs to please me. But I am convinced by
her tone of voice and her descriptions that she has a real emotional
problem and that the ABCs that I am assuming she has are probably
accurate.]

Albert: Now *that's* the evaluation . . .

Susan: [Laughing] My God, that sounds terrible.

[Albert: I immediately assume from her last statement that she probably
has a secondary symptom — that she feels 'terrible' about her negative
evaluation of herself. So I make a note to myself to get back after to
exploring her symptom stress — her symptom about her symptom. But
I first return to her primary symptom — self-downing about her perceived inefficiency as a therapist.]

[Windy: Albert notes here that Susan probably has a meta-emotional
problem (Sequence: Step 5). However, he probably does not want to lose
the momentum that he has achieved at this point of the interview and
thus he keeps his focus on Susan's primary problem. You will note that
Albert does not return to her meta-emotional problem in this interview.]

Albert: That's right, you see. And that's what we want to question,
           and that's why we go to D, disputing. Let's suppose the worst
           again, that your observation is true and let's even suppose
           you go *on* acting this way, you're not very good at therapy as
           they are. How does that make *you*, a human, an ass?

[Albert: I could, of course, question her perception of her being ineffica-
cious as a therapist, but instead I go forward to the more elegant solution of REBT — even if she can provide evidence for this inefficiency,
how does that prove that *she*, an entire *person*, is *an ass*?]

[Windy: Note that Albert does not formally help Susan to connect her
irrational belief with her withdrawal at C (Sequence: Step 8). He probably infers that she understands this. Consequently, he proceeds to the
disputing stage (Sequence: Step 9).]

Susan: I guess somewhere I feel that I *have* to excel at *something*.

[Windy: It is interesting to note that as soon as Albert disputes Susan's
self-downing belief that she comes up with her musturbatory belief.]

Albert: Right. You see the '*have to*'.
Susan: I *have to* excel at something.
Albert: And if you change that '*have to*', to 'I'd *like to* excel at some-
           thing, but if I don't, I don't', would you then feel like an ass?
Susan: No, I wouldn't. But I really have to change the whole state-
           ment anyway. I *have to* excel at *everything*. I want to excel at
           everything I touch.
Albert: Well, but notice you just said two things. I *want to* excel at
           everything', which I think almost every human says, 'I'd *like
           to*', 'I *want to* excel at all *important* things'. Not tiddly-winks,
           you don't care if you don't excel at tiddly-winks, do you?

[Windy: Here Albert helps Susan to distinguish carefully between her
rational belief and her irrational belief.]

Susan: No, that would be all right. *That* would show that I was only
           human.
Albert: Yes, right. But you want to excel at every important thing and
           then you say 'and therefore I *have to*', is that right?
Susan: Yes.
Albert: Now, in REBT we never question desires, preferences, wishes,
           wants, because you could *want* anything. You could want,
           right now, 10 million dollars, or to be the greatest genius at
           therapy in the world, and as long as you were saying 'I *want*
           it, but 'I don't *have it*', you wouldn't be into trouble. But we
           question the '*have to*'. Why *must* you excel at an important
           thing like therapy? Why must you?
Susan: I don't know.
Albert: Well, think about that.

[Albert: I could easily tell her the 'right' answer here. But I prefer that she figure it out herself.]

Susan: Well, I dunno. I suppose . . . er . . . I think it may be that I'm a
            product of growing up where I've been told, or it's been
            implied that if you do something, do it well.

[Windy: Note that Susan doesn't directly respond to Albert's disputing question: 'Why must you excel at an important thing like therapy? Note how Albert responds in his next intervention.]

Albert: Right. Let's suppose that's true. And, incidentally, that has
            sense to it, because if you do something well it would be
            preferable to doing it poorly. We all learn that because that's
            not false. Our parents and our schools and our books teach
            us to 'try to do well. If at once you don't succeed, try, try
            again to succeed.' Isn't that what it means? And so that's OK.
            But we're still asking another question, not why it's *prefer-
            able* to do well, why *must* you do what's preferable. Why do
            you *have to*?

[Windy: Albert shows Susan that her answer to his previous question provides evidence why it is preferable to do well. Then he asks her why she must do what is preferable. This is a typical Ellis intervention.]

Susan: I feel better when I . . . when I *do* accomplish. I feel better
            about myself.
Albert: Ah, about *yourself*. But you see you've just again said two
            things, (1) 'I feel better about *it*,' which we hope is true —
            that you would feel better about accomplishment rather than
            sitting on your rump and doing nothing or doing badly. So
            you'd better feel better about it. But you're saying 'I feel bet-
            ter about *me*, I only accept *me* when I do *it* well.' Now, is *that*
            a legitimate conclusion? 'I can only accept *me*, *myself*, my
            being, my totality, when I do *it*, therapy, well.' Now is that a
            good conclusion?

[Windy: Albert tracks Susan quite carefully here. You will note that he originally disputed her self-downing belief, moved to disputing her demanding belief when she moved to this type of iB and has now gone back to disputing her self-downing belief. My own preference is to help the client to dispute fully one type of iB before moving to a related iB. Thus, I may have helped Susan to dispute her self-downing belief fully before disputing her must.]

Susan: You mean, is it accurate?
Albert: Well, will it give you good results?

[Albert:Actually, her conclusion is poor, meaning unrealistic and illogical. But I want her to see that in REBT we do not *only* show clients that
their thoughts are unrealistic and illogical, but also that they won't
work — will give them poor results.]

[Windy: You will note that Susan and Albert refer to the three criteria for
irrationality — empirical, logical and pragmatic — in very quick succession. My preference here would have been her to slow the pace down so
that Susan could have considered more fully each criterion in turn.]

Susan: No, it won't give me good results.
Albert: It'll give you what you have . . . withdrawal, anxiety. Maybe
            what you said at the beginning of this session, some kind of
            anguish, terror almost, which may be the thing that is making
            you withdraw — which we could just guess about, but it cer-
            tainly *won't give you pleasure* and it won't help you to stay
            with this practicum or any other thing that you enter. You'll
            tend to run away. And by running away will you do as well as
            you'd like to do?
Susan: No.
Albert: You'll normally do worse, isn't that so?
Susan: Well, I will not have accomplished anything at all.
Albert: That's right.
Susan: Except to have reinforced again, once again, Susan strikes
            out.
Albert: That's the irony, you see. That's really an irony. By demanding
            that 'I must do "X" well', such as therapy in a practicum. 'I *have
            to*', 'I *have to*', 'I've *got to*', 'I've *got to* do it *well*', you will *with-
            draw* and not even do it *at all*. You see the *need*, the *necessity*
            of, performing well leads to withdrawal or anxiety, which inter-
            feres with your performance. You see that's catch 22. Now, how
            do you think you can get out of that bind?

[Windy: You will note that Albert focuses on pragmatic disputing of
Susan's irrational beliefs in this sequence.]

Susan: By not withdrawing and not being anxious.
Albert: That's right. First, not withdrawing. Then you still would be
            anxious if you didn't withdraw. Now, how could you get rid of
            your anxiety? Let's assume you stayed with it, and it was
            uncomfortable to stay. And that's what we recommend in
            REBT, to stay with your discomfort until you make yourself

comfortable. *How* could you get rid of the anxiety by staying with your discomfort?

Susan: By applying myself more, and er . . . learning the techniques.

Albert: Right. That's one way, but that's a little inelegant. That would work, because let's suppose that you stayed with it no matter how uncomfortable you felt and you learned the techniques of doing therapy. You got better at it and you felt *unanxious*. Do you realize why that would be an inelegant kind of solution? It would work, temporarily, but why would it only work temporarily? Why would it be inelegant?

[Windy: By using Socratic questioning, Albert is attempting to get Susan to see that the only elegant way of overcoming her withdrawal and the anxiety that underpins her defensive behaviour is to challenge and change her irrational beliefs. He makes this point more explicitly in his next response but one.]

Susan: Because I think it attacks just a very small piece of it.

Albert: That's right. And even in that small piece, suppose you first did well, and then later did badly. Suppose you finished the practicum, learned REBT quite well, as well as anybody does, and then compare yourself with other therapists and *still* do poorly. Then what would you go back to telling yourself?

Susan: That I really don't belong here. I'll go back to the same thing.

Albert: And 'I'm a no-good person for being a no-good therapist.' You see, you haven't got rid of that. So the technique in REBT is, first, *stay* with the uncomfortable situation and then *work* on the anxiety by giving up your *must*. Now, how could you give up, 'I *must* do well', 'I *have to*', 'I've *got to*'?

[Albert: I don't merely allow Susan to *act* well by staying in the uncomfortable therapy situation. I want her to do that *and* to tackle her *must* — to *think* differently *and* act differently.]

Susan: By telling myself, 'OK, I will continue, and I will try, and I will do my best, and if it works out, that will be very nice. And if it doesn't work out, well maybe I'll try another kind of er . . . training.'

Albert: Or . . . 'Maybe I'll . . .'

Susan: I'll go into another field.

Albert: No, no . . . that's OK. Those are OK *practical* solutions. But better yet, 'Maybe I'll stay in this field and not *have* to be so great. It doesn't *have* to work out well — I don't *have* to do as well as the others.' Isn't that better?

[Windy: Susan doesn't fully see that the real psychological solution to her emotional problem is to challenge and change her must. So Albert emphasizes this solution without denigrating her more practically oriented solutions.]

Susan: Yes. I can be a student, a C student, and survive.

Albert: I often talk about the Sunday painters. They're out in the park with their easels and their paints every Sunday, painting some of the most *god-awful* things, and some of them know it and they *still* enjoy painting. Now how do they *continue* to paint those *god-awful* things and still enjoy it? What are they telling themselves?

[Windy: Here Ellis is using a metaphor to reinforce his point (see DiGiuseppe, 1991).]

Susan: One . . . they *like* those god-awful things.

Albert: Right.

Susan: And two, there's nothing wrong with those god-awful things.

Albert: Or better — there's nothing wrong with *them* for painting god-awfully. You see. And they even might say 'I don't like my paintings, but I like the *painting*.' They're doing poorly at the activity but allowing themselves to *enjoy* it. I always quote the statement of Oscar Wilde, 'Anything that's worth doing is worth doing *badly*.' You see? Because the *activity itself* is worth it. The *results* may *not* be worth it. You may never like the *results*. Now, as a therapist, we wouldn't want you to go on being a really bad therapist. And, as you said before, 'Maybe I'd better get into another field or something like that.' But that would be later when you've really determined that you're bad at therapy. First, you stay with your discomfort, as I said. Then you recognize that you are *creating* much of it. You *make* yourself anxious. Third, you see that you mainly do it by your *'have to'*, your *'got to'*, your *'must'*. And by 'I am a rotten person if I do badly, rottenly.' Then you *dispute*: 'Where is the evidence that I'm a rotten person or that I *have* to do well'? And what conclusion do you end up with then?

[Albert: I persist at trying to help Susan get to her *core* dysfunctional belief — that she *must* be good at therapy and is a *rotten person* if she does not do as well as she *must*.]

Susan: I'm beginning to wonder, am I really saying that I am a rotten person or am I really and truly saying, I am a rotten therapist?

Albert: Well, let's suppose you were. Let's suppose *that* for the moment. That would be . . . that might be sane. If you had enough evidence, if you did poorly time and again, and if you're not that good at therapy and you're concluding 'I am *rotten* at *therapy* and I'll never be more than average or mediocre at therapy', then that would be OK. But I doubt whether you'd withdraw from doing therapy so *quickly* if that were *so*.

Susan: Aaaah.

Albert: You see?

Susan: Aaaah.

Albert: Do you really have evidence?

Susan: I was going to say, I really needed evidence. I see. That I can understand.

Albert: You see, just like those Sunday painters. They might go week after week, 52 weeks of the year, to the park and paint, and then finally say, 'You know, I like the painting but I don't like the result. Maybe I'd better do sculpture. I would get better results.' That would be OK. But if they quit after the first week then we get suspicious of their self-downing. How do they even know they're right about their *painting* but not about *themselves* being no good. You see?

[Windy: By continuing to use the Sunday painter metaphor, Albert helps Susan to see that her defensive withdrawal prevents her from identifying, challenging and changing her irrational beliefs.]

Susan: I know you might find it very difficult to believe, but at home I have now sitting umm . . . some paint and some canvases [laughing]. Because my daughter is getting me ready for retirement. She said, 'Gee, you've always said you'd like to paint.' I have not touched the paints for two months because . . . why? Because I know when I get to it the painting's gonna be lousy.

Albert: And it *should* right from the start be great?

Susan: Be terrific! Right.

Albert: Now isn't *that* something you're imposing on yourself? And you see it was interesting that I used painting as an example, and now it turns out that you're really in the position of copping out. But that's a good thing, because in therapy you'd at least have the excuse. 'Well if I'm rotten at therapy, I'd better not be a therapist because I might harm others.' Or something like that. But in painting, *who would you harm*? If you really work for weeks and months at it and it turned out that

you were no good at it, who would be harmed? Would anybody be harmed?

[Windy: Albert now helps Susan to begin to generalize her learning
about the role of her irrational beliefs from the therapy situation to
painting (Sequence: Step 13).]

Susan: No.
Albert: And you would have *learned* at least the valuable information
           that, 'You know, painting may not *be* my cup of tea.' You
           would have *gathered* some evidence. Now in cases like yours,
           you're withdrawing too *quickly* and therefore we probably
           could call it defensive. But don't accept that you are defensive
           because I think you are or some other therapists think you
           are. We could be *wrong*. You might be very perceptive and
           sense quickly that you're not that good at therapy and decide
           to do something else. That would be legitimate. But *get the
           evidence*. You see? And the quicker you withdraw from doing
           therapy, the less evidence you'll have, you see?

[Albert: I am using evidence and logic here to try to show Susan that she
is not necessarily wrong to withdraw from therapy but that her withdrawing *so quickly* tends to show that she *may* be avoiding self-downing about her feeling. I am not trying to prove that she *is* defensively
withdrawing but only that she *may be*. My interpretation could be
wrong. So I do not want to foist it on her.]

[Windy: An important part of REBT is encouraging clients to think for
themselves and not to accept what their therapists say because they are
therapists.]

Susan: Yeah, that's er . . .
Albert: Anything else you wanted to raise about this?
Susan: No . . . I think that . . . er, this is something I really have to, er
           . . . give a lot of thought to. Because it's, er . . . I . . . [sighing]
           I think this is the first time I feel that I'm down to the kernel.
           And, er . . . and I *could* do as I have done all these years, say,
           'OK, terrific, that was a great session', and go out and have
           lunch and forget about it. But I'm gonna make myself sit on
           that kernel and chew on that kernel.
Albert: That's right . . .
Susan: . . . And unfold. Try to unfold.
Albert: And that's a very good point you're making. *Don't* assume
           that what I said was correct because I said it or because I have

some status. See whether it applies to you and test it out, keep testing, you see.

Susan: Yeah. Uh-hum. [Bell rings] Was that the end?

Albert: No. That just happened to be the bell to open the door downstairs.

Susan: Because I feel very well satisfied that I have gotten quite a . . . quite a jolt here.

Albert: Now, how can you *use* that jolt to your benefit? That's the main thing.

[Albert: No matter how much insight she seems to be getting, I want to try to see that she *uses* it to work against her self-downing, her defensiveness, and her withdrawal, and her basic musts that lie behind these feelings and actions, and to *change* them.]

Susan: [Sighing]. Well, I think what I'm gonna do is sit down at home and go over the past year or so of events where I have tried to do something and er . . . they have not worked out . . . none of them has worked out and see whether indeed they have not worked out because I realistically evaluated it *or* er . . . I didn't give it enough time.

[Windy: Susan is suggesting to herself a homework assignment to test for herself the validity of Albert's hypothesis (Sequence: Step 11). Albert thus does not need to make the point that one way in which she can deepen her learning is by the use of homework assignments. Thus, he does not need to introduce Step 10 of the sequence.]

Albert: Withdrew too quickly. Right.

Susan: Which was something that was brought up yesterday too er . . . or, if . . . Have I given the things I have turned my hand to enough time and effort?

Albert: Right. That's a good point.

Susan: Because in my case there was plenty of time, but I don't know how much effort went into these activities.

Albert: Yeah. Because if you're telling yourself what we said before, let's just assume we're right, 'I *must* do well and isn't it awful if I don't.' And, 'If not, I might be a rotten therapist or even a rotten person.' If so, you may force yourself to continue at therapy and not really give it your *all*. So, the test of whether you're good at *anything* is: (1) take enough time, don't withdraw, and then (2) really throw yourself in and take it as a *challenge* to learn. You see? If you really are bad at something you still have the challenge of doing better. It's an interesting puzzle to solve if you take that attitude. Like, people don't play tic-tac-toe because it's too easy. Some of them don't even play chequers because it is too easy, so they play chess, or Go, or some complicated game, *knowing* they're going to lose but it's a greater challenge. Now you . . . this is your life, let's see if you can take the *challenge* of finding out whether quitting therapy is a cop-out on your part, which we're not sure about yet, because it could be. Or whether you are quickly ascertaining whether therapy is not for you. But give it more time, give it more effort, stop *must*urbating about it and then we'll see.

[Albert:I do not want her immediately to stop doing therapy — or to decide to continue doing it. I would like her to *consider* the hypotheses we have raised about her history of failing and about her consequently defensively withdrawing. I hope that she *experiments* more, without musturbating, to see what her final conclusion about being a therapist might be.]

Susan: Yeah. Fine.
Albert: You see now what you can do?
Susan: Yeah. That will be my homework.
Albert: Yes. That will be your homework. To *consider* what we've said and test it as a hypothesis. It's *only* a hypothesis, and see whether you can find evidence for either your appropriately getting out of a situation, or running out pell-mell *de-fen-sive-ly*.
Susan: Yeah. And even as I now think, as you're talking, of the events of the past year or two, it's amazing to me that my conclusions always were 'Well, I am not, I am *not*, I am *not*' and so I dropped all of those efforts. Because I thought, 'I am *not*.'
Albert: But you could have said, 'Maybe I am not.' Let's see.
Susan: Yeah.
Albert: Right?
Susan: Right.
Albert: OK. You work on that.
Susan: Fine. Very good.
Albert: All right?
Susan: Well, I appreciate that.

[Albert:I thought that this was a good initial session — which gave Susan some important things to *consider* and *think* about. Her being a therapist probably helped her get some of my points quickly — and perhaps be able to *act* on them. But, even if she were an accountant, an attorney, or something else, I would have proceeded as I did, but with much more detail, explanations and examples. I still, however, would have tried to make the main point about her musts and self-downing leading to her possible defensiveness and too ready withdrawal.]

Afterword

If you have found it instructive to read and study the transcripts that appear in this book with their accompanying commentary, you may also find the following two books of interest:

Ellis, A. (1971). Growth through reason. Hollywood, CA: Wilshire Books.

This book contains verbatim transcripts of regular sessions of REBT conducted by Albert Ellis, Ben Ard, Maxie Maultsby and other well-known REBT therapists. Ongoing commentaries are provided. Although the book is 25 years old and thus reflects the practice of REBT of its day, it is still a useful publication.

Dryden, W. and Yankura, J. (1992). Daring to be Myself: A Case Study of Rational-emotive Therapy. Buckingham: Open University Press.

This book contains verbatim transcripts and analysis of portions of a 10-session therapy that I conducted in the early 1980s. It also contains portions of a follow-up session that took place nine months later and an interview with the client about her impressions of the therapy eight years on.

For further details of training opportunities in REBT contact:

Centre for REBT
156 Westcombe Hill
Blackheath
London SE3 7DX
Tel: 0181 293 4114

Professor Windy Dryden
Course Director: MSc REBT
Department of Psychology
Goldsmiths College
New Cross
London SE14 6NW
Tel: 0171 919 7872

References

Bard JA (1980). Rational-emotive Therapy in Practice. Champaign, IL: Research Press.

Bordin ES (1979). The generalizability of the psychoanalytic concept of the working alliance.Psychotherapy: Theory, Research and Practice 16: 252–260.

DiGiuseppe R (1984). Thinking what to feel. British Journal of Cognitive Psychotherapy 2(1): 27–33.

DiGiuseppe R (1991). Comprehensive cognitive disputing in rational-emotive therapy. In M Bernard (Ed.) Using Rational-emotive Therapy Effectively. New York: Plenum.

Dryden W (1986a). Vivid methods in rational-emotive therapy. In A Ellis and RM Grieger (Eds) Handbook of Rational-emotive Therapy, Vol 2. New York: Springer.

Dryden W (1986b). Language and meaning in rational-emotive therapy. In W Dryden and P Trower (Eds) Rational-emotive Therapy: Recent Developments in Theory and Practice. Bristol: Institute for RET (UK).

Dryden W (1990). Rational-emotive Counselling in Action. London: Sage.

Dryden W (1994). Overcoming Guilt. London: Sheldon.

Dryden W (1995a). Preparing for Client Change in Rational Emotive Behaviour Therapy. London: Whurr.

Dryden W (1995b). Facilitating Client Change in Rational Emotive Behaviour Therapy. London: Whurr.

Dryden W and Yankura J (1993). Counselling Individuals: A Rational-emotive Handbook. London: Whurr.

Dryden W and Yankura J (forthcoming). Treatment Techniques in Rational Emotive Behaviour Therapy. London: Whurr.

Ellis A (1983). The philosophic implications and dangers of some popular behavior therapy techniques. In M Rosenbaum, CM Franks and Y Jaffe (Eds) Perspectives in Behavior Therapy in the Eighties. New York: Springer.

Ellis A (1984). How to Maintain and Enhance your Rational-emotive Therapy Gains. New York: Institute for Rational-Emotive Therapy.

Ellis A (1985). Overcoming Resistance: Rational-emotive Therapy with Difficult Clients. New York: Springer.

Ellis A (1994). Reason and Emotion in Psychotherapy. Revised and updated edition. New York: Birch Lane Press.

Horvath AO and Greenberg LS (Eds) (1994). The Working Alliance: Theory, Research and Practice. New York: Wiley.

Gendlin ET (1978). Focusing. New York: Everest House.

Passons W (1975). Gestalt Approaches in Counselling. New York: Holt, Rinehart and Winston.

Trexler LD (1976). Frustration is a fact, not a feeling. Rational Living 11(2): 19–22.

Walen SR, DiGiuseppe R and Dryden W (1992). A Practitioner's Guide to Rational-emotive Therapy, 2nd edn. New York: Oxford University Press.

Index